THE APOCRYPHON

OF

THE DISPOSSESSED

KOLADE FOLAMI

Printed in the United States of America

Imperial Publishers Limited

Ibadan.

For Mama 'Nike Ademuyiwa

INTRODUCTION

Here is the secret writing,
The record of the orphans of history,
The roaming ghosts of the place of the
shifting cemetery.

The canary has arrived,
The loquacious bird,
The canary has perched,
The talkative bird,
'Death is not apportioned to me,'
Is the song of the canary.   10
Power dispossessed,
Chicanery was contrived.

Who approaches the dilemma of the
three-path junction?

The meeting place of the elders,
Or the dales at the tip of no return?
The earth's a place of commerce,
We come and we return.
But they sought power,
that they might be masters of men,   20
and sought to become the earth's

permanent residents.

The peacock struts in majesty,
He told one, he told all,
He told all comers that he has the
Mandate of heaven,
For this, they bowed before the peacock,
But the night came and even the
Peacock must
Find the place of sleep.   30

But for some, sleep is elusive,
Like the puffing adder, prevented entry to
The tranquil waters of heaven.

Steve *Biko*,[1] Steve please,
The comrades have found a shade under
The awning of the ones who cudgeled
Bagged prisoner with spiked clubs,
Spiked clubs in the hypogeal death chambers,
Where dank mist muffled painful bleats,
Or the howls of the unfortunate dissidents.   40
Steve *Biko*, Steve, please.

Chieftaincy circulates,
It goes round and reaches all,
For the stability of their paradise,
They constructed hell,

---

[1] Steve Biko, South African apartheid activist who was murdered by the apartheid
state agents while in their custody.

v

They ringfenced heaven,
And made damnation a spectacle.
But the occupants of hell assailed heaven's gates,
And the bloodhounds of paradise
Assured one another of mutual   50
destruction.

The world of men is joyless,
Yet the road to it is the busiest,
And at its ports cacophony never cease,
Only if the ecstatic arrival sees the drawn face
of departure,
Maybe the return shuttle would be boarded
Before clearing the customs of the womb,
But then, even twins have unsimilar
destinies,   60
Therefore, enjoy your stay.

The world is a whip,
It swings to the front,
It swings to the back.
The world is a wind,
It wastes itself in whirling effluence.
The world is a mystery,
The wisest have not figured it out.
When the evening arrives,
Let hot bath meet sweet lullaby,   70
And let those who know,
Steal a quick nap on the soft
bosom of the temporary lover.

Come hither, come closer,
Let the musical speech of
The talking drum enliven your feet,
And the rattle of the tambourine
Fill your waist with mirth.

Pestilence visited the country
Like the fire of the wild, it spread.   80
The borders were locked
And the streets were cleared of loitering bodies.
The citizens saw pestilence in the streets,
And hunger inside the houses.
Pestilence is outside and hunger is inside.
This time around, even the husbands of the nation
Filed for divorce and rejected custody rights.

Here is the secret writing of the ones marooned
from history,
That they may embrace sleep,   90
And the marketplace of nether roamers
shall be deserted.

TABLE OF CONTENTS

TIES THAT NEVER BIND

The moonlit night used to bring us together,
Did it really bring us together?
We were told there were ties that bind,
Or which bound us together like the hundred
broomsticks,
Or were we merely forced to coexist?
By the necessity of banding?
By the love for harmony?
Harmony like the opening of orchids in autumn,
Indeed, desirable and, no doubt, beautiful-   10
to every beholder who craved truthful beauties,
or the ephemeral.

The winding bush paths used to bring us together,
We trudged and filed with songs in our lips,
Like hummingbirds, our tunes the forest came alive
But were we in an accord?
Did we achieve concord?
Or were we simply forced to tolerate one another?
Today is the final day and no more
procrastination,   20
The friend that we enlisted in the cooperative
clearing of virgin forests,
Will you show up or we find another in your stead?

We were happy in each other's company,
But how did we become ensnarer of brothers?
Snatcher of maidenhoods at the same bush paths
which
Forked to the streams and the farms?
The cries could be heard in the hamlets as the
Earthenware pots were smashed on rocks,   30
To be found later by the curious brushes or
picks of the archaeologist,
450 Before Present was the precise date without the
story,
Another curio for the gazing pleasure-
Of those who will never know why the pot was
broken.

It is tempting and very enticing,
There is nothing as sweetening to the palate
as-   40
The gathering in fluorescent-lit rotundas
Or in digital amphitheatres to tell ourselves that
Carpetbaggers from the Maghreb and buccaneers
from across the Atlantic,
Came with scimitars and swords to take apart what
bound us together,
But can the lizard have an abode in the wall without
the presence of the crevice?

THE SONG OF THE RED FLECKED PARROT

The red-flecked parrot,
　　The denizen of topless palm trees,
　　The red-flecked parrot,
Lone ditty coursed from the hardened beak,
"The world rejected the truth"
The song of the red-flecked parrot,
"The truth is orphaned"
The lone ditty from the hardened beak.

Nothing but a battlefield is life,
The world! Nothing but a battlefield,　　　　　10
Dear lad, your noonday began but it was
benighted,
Oh lass you mourn,
For your morn was permanently eclipsed
By the envious fiends in the gab of friends
Deep Life! Troublous existence,
But you claimed it was a marketplace?
Yes, it is a marketplace,

For we came for a mere exchange
And we return home at dusk.   20

It is also a place of strife,
The citadel of noisome pestilence,
The empire of sharpened daggers on the jugular,
The university of frustrated ambitions,
The shopping-mall of polished vanity,
The babel of musical cacophony,
The dungeon of restless apparitions,
The Golgotha of bleached skulls,
The valley of hushed despondency,
The autobahn to happily-never-after!   30
The partridge's apparel is unchanging,
Season to season, same nondescript plumes,
Nothing distinguishing and nothing remarkable,
The world loved you oh partridge-person!

Like a buffoon in the marketplace,
Your antic is a pleasant sight,
The apparels of previous years are not changed,
No greatness and all listlessness,
Your lethargy is taken for humility
And your poverty is assumed to be piety.   40

The world loves you oh partridge-person!

The lack of culture made the country person
To enter the city cladded in loin-clothes,
But the country-folks say theirs is the
Existence of the city dukes in wild rusticity,

Untaxed venison of the woods,
Graciously accompanied on the palate with
Early morning palm wine that is far away from the
foaming bubbles.

With peace bequeathed by **Olodumare**,[2]   50
"Ours is the existence of city dukes in wild
rusticity"

No marvel greater than the piety of the strippers,
The year goes to its end and all the
Faithful assembled
At the Abbey of the Holy Paraclete,
All are called and none are judged,
The arrival of the three in the vestry
The carriage is all penitent,
Wistfully supplicant,   60
Janus faced is the ending and the beginning,
The old departed and the new arrived,
We have all resolved to leave evil,
We have all decided to start new with new,
No marvel is greater than the piety of the strippers,
To the abattoirs of nubile fleshes they returned,
After the new year had been committed to the hands
of a higher power.

The world is a battlefield, but you came to
party,   70

---

[2] The Supreme God of the Yoruba. He is believed to be reachable through
intermediary gods.

You traded fatigues for dinner tuxes,
They told you to beat swords to ploughshares
But they kept daggers hidden in velvet gloves,
They preached peace and gave benediction,
but they rehearsed death with titillating finesse
Martial music was masked with the tempo of a
lullaby
The dainties of the dinner-table,
A preparation by enemies in the presence of
friends,   80
The world is a battlefield, but you came to
party.

Darkness is the friend of evil deeds,
"Let there be light" says the most high,
But their ways are wicked hence they darkened
the sun,
And made the moon succumb
To slumber in the hands of Morpheus
Suckling babes are snatched at deserted
alleys,   90
Pubescent innocence is ravished in the dark
arenas,
While returning from early recruitment into the
hunt for vanishing dough.

The world is a battlefield, but you came to party.

THE AUTOPSY

PART I

Our enemy is the truth,
For this reason, we remain in chains.
The chains were long, neck to neck,
Sombre, forlorn towards a never to end furlough
In the wilderness of gritted teeth,
I heard your cries beneath the Atlantic, dear
Restless comrades,
Shortly, I shall attend to your summons,
For now, the concern is for the present,
Even though the present is the offspring of   10
the pangs of the past,
I heard you and it was clear,
I saw you for I chose not to be blind,
You have always been around,
You have never left,
Your loud wailing till the end of time,
But your descendants gave the middle finger,
And deadened your anguished cries with the din
of the recent.

Ours is the destiny of conquest,   20
We have made our brothers our enemy,
It is an old war, but we painted it recent and
told ourselves it was new,
We repeated the lie that it was the first time
That we made the skulls of our brethren the tiles of
the palaces.

Male, tribal marks, 5 feet 2 inches,
Military officer as identified by the army authorities,
Single gunshot wound and the manner of
death is homicide,   30
Dear Mr. Medical Examiner,
The commander calls
You say you are busy with divination,
If your divination proclaims good tidings
And the commander declares damnation,
Which one do you think will supersede?
The cause of death is not homicide,
For the Supreme Headquarters,
It is 'blast and penetrating injuries due to
explosion of aircraft.'   40

FLASHBACK:

Brigadier Taju you have your marching orders,
The new aero power shall brook no discrimination,
No civilian and no combatant,
All are enemies and the war from the air shall be
total.

8

Total war and total death,
Brothers and sisters,
Napalm for evening births,
Shrapnel for supper,
Brigadier Taju you have your marching 50
orders.
Annihilation is the plan,
Extermination is the objective
Brigadier, you are not allowed any dissent,
Obey the last order
Ilyushin and **Mikoyan MiG,**
Hell from the heavens,
Death on the earth,
Nothing must be left standing
No one must be left 60
To bear tales of stupidity
No journalist and no red cross,
No crescent and no eavesdropper,
Hell from heaven, waste on the earth.

I, Brigadier Taju, shall be true to the laws
Of war,

Where is soldiery when babies are bathed with
fiery thunders?

Where is chivalry where maidens are sent to
Sheol in the noon of existence? 70

Where is the courage in the desolation of
Madrasahs and Cathedrals?

Brigadier Taju obey the last order,
They have made their choice of death,
Ours is to provide the transport to the desired
destination.

Let your dragons take to the skies,
Let their breaths draw in oxygen to cook up
incendiary,
And at your word let hell be rained on those   80
Who found it difficult to know their place!

PRESENT TIME:

Professional ethics call for truth,
It will take the legions of hell to browbeat the
Brave to submission,
Murder I shall write and a bullet traveling through
The temple is the cause.

The love for the thunder deity is always forced,
Ours is the power and dominion,
We shall dictate and you shall write,
We shall give the word and you shall stamp,
Accident via copter-crash you shall write!   90
Tick-Tock, Tick-Tock,
Minutes formed hours
Hours formed days.

The hen perched on the line,
The line complained not of pains,
The hen felt no discomfort,

Compensating tension and nothing more,
But the hen did not see the trained gaze of the hunter,
It did not see itself in the crosshairs of the
slinger. 100

The one whose head balanced unknown load,
Oh, what a sorry sight,
He carried gourds and porcelains,
Oh, what a sorry sight,
He carried large earthenware, the father of cooking pots,
Oh, what a sorry sight.

FLASHBACK:

An embarrassment in person is Brigadier
Taju, 110
Modification of orders,
What effrontery? What confidence?
Supreme Headquarters of supremo supremacy!
The order was a blitzkrieg
The execution was a target-shooting
Sack Taju and lose his tribe
New orders and with express dispatch:
Compromise Taju!

Repeat: Compromize Taju!

PRESENT TIME:

The commitment to the truth remained   120
unshakable,
The body of evidence screamed single gunshot
wound
From an outside trusted finger,
The report's finished and addressed,
The commitment to the truth remains unshakable,
Harsh Stentorian: Open the door now!
"Who are you?"
"These are the authorities, Open the door
now!"   130
Beads of perspiration mixed with
trepidation stiffened the limbs,
A loud bang and wooden doors flew from
the hinges,
Nothing was taken and nothing was stolen,
A twosome came to deliver a message from above,
'Dr. Adeyemo!'
The silenced-beretta coughed,
Crimson blood flowed from the
Path made by the projectile through the   140
forehead.

Brigadier Taju served the nation meritoriously,
A woman wept profusely, and a lad
gazed confusedly,
Closed and sealed the inert body,
The truth shall remain interred till eternity.

PART II

EXCHANGE:

Dear Journalist Kayode,
Your meddlesomeness was globally known,
"All powers must be held accountable"
A riposte from trained lips.

The dead have no business conversing with
the living,
But for you, I make an exception,
It is your lot to do your own post-mortem,
Now grab an apron and start dissecting,
"Many have been coming all these years"   10
"The only person I trusted was the lawyer"
"The lawyer who thought the law was all"

Interjection: Did you not also think the truth
is all?

"Now don't you ever interrupt me again"
"Now your presence is getting burdensome"
"You are welcome to be a guest of the netherworld"
"Styx beckons, cross it and join us here"
Journalist Kayode, I come when I come,
Your cemetery has been shifting,   20
You have cried yourself hoarse,

Shouting for a justice that never came,
Your murderers lived happily ever after,
They married new wives,
Got new titles and enjoyed their loot in peace,
They read bedtime stories to precocious
Grandchildren,
You wept for the children you never saw,
You wept for the dreams that never came
through,   30
You wept for the lovers that you left without
blankets,
You wept for the mother who saw your beginning
and your end,
You wept and cried yourself hoarse for thirty years,
But your friends quelled your noise with the din of
merriment,
Grab an apron and let's start your post-mortem,
"I don't have time for nonsense"
Guffaw! You immortals have all the time in   40
eternity,
I am not one of those who trended your names
To incite guilt or show activism,
I am here to hear your side of the story,
Therefore, Journalist Kay grab an apron NOW!
"Yes sir"

"It was blown out from the middle-torso"
"A memory relived for nightmare benefits"
"Tomb-raider, grave-disturber"
"Endoskeleton under ill-fitting suit"   50

"The lid had been closed since we left the mortician's"

But you were at the interment at Arechi?

"I was there, no one saw me"
Are you sure?
"Segun Ray saw me"
"He knew I was to be killed,"
The friendship of the magpie and the pyracantha,
You had berries but did not see the hunger
of your friends,   60
You confronted the sword with the pen,
The sword made inks of the brave's blood,
And with money, friends call the hero a villain,
Bring Jasmine in its whitish-pink splendour,
Thirty years have not removed the stink,
"For me it is Delphinium,
Cheerfulness comes before fragrance in the house of
hades"

You have been like me and I'm yet unlike
you,   70
But for a concession to us, let Daphne sprout
in this nether midsummer,
cheerfulness for your tired soul and fragrance for my
choked lungs.

"The Dragon belched upon the lower torso"
"Like daylight, clear to the blind"
"If your ghoulish thirst is sated,

Your departure shall be the gospel."

The tour to the sepulchre is deeply
appreciated,   80
Ravens and Crows' guano on marble
headstone,
But the autopsy has only begun,
The earth is not the place of justice,
Like the canary's, your song is desired,
Oh, a melancholic tone of the nightingale is
preferred,
Now sing for the one who has ears for the
Sad lyrics of the dispossessed,
Please, sing and say your truth dear cardinal   90
of the dark.

JOURNALIST KAY:

At the depth of hades lies **Apaadi** the place of
potsherd,
The justice of the earth, a vanishing point,
The vengeance of the netherworld only for the early
arrivals,
Weeping started at the departure of the mourners,
They forgot and I remained the memory
unobliterated,
"We are not only in the office but also in   100
power"
 His **khakistocratic** majesty announced to those
who had ears,
The masquerade had ears,

The homing dog had ears, also, for the hunter's
whistle,
The gunshots were heard,
The dictator came to war against his nation,
All were hostages, all were criminals,
All were suspects, all were convicts,   110
Khakistocratic majesty ascended the
throne,
History has no innocent bystander,
Khakistocratic wanted to be Pharaoh,
But he thought not of immortality and
He built no pyramids,
For the sake of hunger, the pelican had a pouched
beak,
Power gave adulation and charm before the
kill,   120
Power feted and I applauded,
Like Chrysanthemum which moved from
The Forbidden City to Kyoto,
Power blanketed iron fist with embroidered silks,
For this reason, I cladded power in borrowed
raiment,
 Like pampered inmates of the dark dungeons,
The realm had a fourth estate and
We believed the self-evident lie,
A prophet shouted himself hoarse,   130
"Army arrangement"[3] he declared,
But I arrived at the devil's dinner with the longest
spoon,

---

[3] Fela Anikulapo Kuti[1985], *Army Arrangement* [LP]

The devil entered the confessional,
It gave sacrament and asked for ultimate devotion,
I asked for a price for the sale of soul,
I am not innocent, and history has no saints,
Only beatified apostates.

Power does not negotiate with prey,
Power takes and gives with all abandon,   140
The buxom hyrax visited the panther's
lodge,
The dog that confabbed with the lion
Shall be birthed in the blood of its arteries,
I digress, sweet-smelling Erica!
Mortality is sorely missed,
The temporariness of swallows in summer,
The focus of the condor on undulating shrubberies
For the fleeting squirrel,
The prancing of the frustrated lynx,   150
Perpetuation of the hunter-hunted dyad,
Yet the violet blooms of Erigeron amidst bulrushes,
Or the euphoria of Euphorbia,
Says life is hope and hope is life,
It is this, with mortality that is sorely missed.

The matter at hand beckons,
Like the Dodo, truth lovers have long ended
On the supper-table of the sons of men,
Many gunslingers and sell-swords trudged
The palace of his **Khakistocratic** Majesty,   160
But in guns lay the diminution of absolute
power,

For how the gun can make supine a citizenry that
Used gunpowder for snuff is the stuff of
wonderment.
The Leviathan had no foreign battles to fight,
Hence its turning inward to cudgel the bush-rats,
So much hell without brimstones,
Let the matter be unraveled,
Even in death honour was not wanting,   170
The ant wagged a finger at the grizzly bear,
The subsequent crush after the sting matters not,
The apparel loaned to power was declared fit for
receivership,
The General asked for the robes of the Khalifa,
Like the fabled Hawk, he approached the sun
To look in the eye the fiery face of the almighty,
He declared himself unquestionable
And all occupants of the ivory tower
Deposited wisdom in the temple of a brute   180
dullard,
But even with absolute power, General
Khakistocracy
Ceased not from frequenting the alleys which
demons avoid,
I was the only witness,
For this, I was marked for death.

RESPONSE:

'Tis true what you said,
History has no innocent bystanders,

Truth or lies are of no value here at the   190
banks of Styx,
'Alleys which demons avoid' is another covering for
murderers.

JOURNALIST KAYODE:

Grotesque, stranger than fiction,
Ermine robes covered tattered ragamuffins,
High-way robbers ensconced in the holy of holies,
But the citadel was founded on skulls hence its daily
acceptance of blood,
They left gun-slinging for money-changing,
I am no bearded Rabbi and I carry no whip,   200
House of power was no place of prayer,
No desecration and even if there was,
The people have been shocked till their
unshockability,
Hence no newness under the sun,
They made a second house for the money changers,
Sorry, only one person sells money to the long
queues of buyers,
Strictly by invitation, to buy in the second
house,   210
The underhand dealings were seen,
The second house of moneychangers, the
road to
Crisp Benjamins for *General Khakistocracy*.

An example must be made, and a lesson must be
taught,

The till is the General's,
Free speech and free question in the republic of
serfs? Unheard of!
In the national interest, the construction of
the second house of foreign money,   220
Never the experiment by God-like mortals
who shall never fail,
The singing canary must be silenced,
Not because he uncovered the dark secrets of the
powerful,
But as an example, to those who fail to mind their
own business.

RESPONSE:

In short, you were offered up as a burnt offering.
Sacrificed to the behemoth that suffocates
all,   230
Scapegoated to the Leviathan
Who craved absolute control of hearts and minds?
Who sought to make men dead
By keeping silent in the face of tyranny.
The fiery transition was not the tragedy,
Before you, many were baptized with napalm at
eventide,
Others were fed with bullets at matins,
But you were the patron saint of
bombarded souls of the suburbia,   240
The helpless angel of the hapless heads
Who collided with the friendly cannonballs,

The agony uncle of unwilling arrivals in the house of
hades,
Transported kicking and screaming by the sentinels
Who swore oaths of allegiance to all sentient
inmates,
Of the unyielding carapace of spatial sovereignty.
But you were no Prometheus,
Why did you incur the Olympian wrath?   250

JOURNALIST KAYODE:

I am no Prometheus,
But I have never betrayed philosophy,
And the ultimate is the freedom of speech.
Yet I told one and all,
That the world hated the truth
And truth-bearers, the armed invaders of the
forbidden city.

Even though to mother truth I have sworn
allegiance,
The quest for freedom of speech shall not be   260
tainted
With the arrogance of the mandarin.

But as for the wearers of borrowed ermines,
The majesties who lilliputianized their brethren,
The new imperators of diminutive estates,
Who, like the peacock, strutted upon the skulls of
unfortunate destinies,
All intentions are criminal liabilities,

No one is truly pure
Except he who chose the silence of the   270
lambs,
Yet even the lambs are led to the slaughter,
Therefore, the ermined butcher
And his acolytes in the abattoir
Are the only innocents in the city
Where all are deemed criminals.

Peacocky Pahlavi,[4]
King of kings without the grace of Cyrus,
Master of masters without the freedom of
Darius,   280
Susa disappeared with Xerxes,
But for Reza the glories of the old
Can be resurrected with SAVAK[5],
But the enemy is no longer outside the walls,
Freedom vanished and no Persian could weave rug
in peace.

But no greater tragedy than the crucifixion of the
truth,
The truth is too pure, and its bearer must
die,   290
There were perfectly made plans to escape

---

[4] Mohammad Reza Pahlavi[1919-1980], former Shah of Persia[now Iran]. He was overthrown in the Irania Revolution of 1979.

[5] The secret police organization established and used by Shah Pahlavi to silence dissidents, torture and kill persons perceived as enemies of the Pahlavi regime. It was disbanded in the heat of the 1979 revolution.

noon-day death,
Somoza gave the word and Stewart died in the
service of the truth[6],
This I saw and for this, I made plans to carry on the
bosom
Laughing grandchildren and to tend potted daisies
or billbergia nutans,
Or the pinks of Bergenia swayed by the
summer breeze   300
Amidst the Sweet Alyssum on the
balustrade,
No thought of being a maroon in Elysium.
Truth is vanity and vanity, truth!

No illusion, for ours is a daily visit to the place of
warfare,
Armed with nothing but a recorder, diary, and pen,
Money is thrown in the face
While poverty crouched in recent memory,
In the dark recesses of the mind lay   310
entombed lack.

For this the mirth was unrivaled,

---

[6] Bill Stewart, the 37-year-old American T.V journalist who was killed in 1979 in Nicaragua by a government soldier. The killing which was filmed by other members of T.V crew was believed to have been influenced by the President of Nicaragua's radio station reportage which accused foreign correspondents of having subversive sympathies in the Nicaraguan civil war. The President in power during the time was Anastasio Somoza. Alongside Stewart, his Nicaraguan interpreter was also executed. They were killed because they were seen to be filming the operations of the government's security forces in a Nicaraguan neighbourhood during the civil war.

When lazy sleuths wrote on the charge sheet:
socialist revolutionary.

The ink was my blood and the pen my gun.
The compliment fattened the ego,
When the importation of Kalashnikovs was
The Hors D'oeuvres served by the blood hounds
Of the imperial city.

Marx was elegant but in the early morning
poverty,   320
A socialist recruit was lost to the craving
For comforting luxuries,
The teenage days was shoeless,
Barefooted I hawked cornmeal at dawn,
A vow was made to take custom
To all shoemakers of kings in all capitals of the
world.

RESPONSE AND EXCHANGE:

Marxist you were not,
When the pay was good
You pitched a tent in the capitalist   330
forecourt,
Yet you were tied to the stake
And burnt as a heretic!

However, not a singularity was your case,
Indeed, your former paymaster who made friends
with the tiger,

Eventually ended up inside its belly at dinner time.
"All are deemed preys in the city of the sabre-tooths"
Animals in human skin, they were called by
the famed apparition.   340

"Once, I told the emperor that if detainees
had a choice
Of their dungeons, the prison would be preferred.
For the prison had humanity,
And the police jail had bestiality.

For the police, theirs is the arcane joy
In the spectacle of the suffering of the captives.
Harassment elevated to a high art!

For the police's nocturnal visits,
The night of the *Jumat* is favored mostly[7],   350
That the unfortunate might be locked
Beyond the legally required twenty-four hours.
The memory of youthful penury,
Resurrected like a poorly interred ghost
Inside the darkness and putridity of *Alagbon*
Cul de sac,
The price for telling it as it is,
In the service of a benighted populace."
When were we ever free?
Elders spent twilight years lying,   360
Wistfully recalling halcyon times that never

---

[7] Night of Every Friday in Nigeria is usually favoured by the police for random arresting of people in the streets.

were,
Foisting the verisimilitude of the recent,
On a present that is too lazy
To check the texts for the unceasing appearance,
Of an ancient Apollyon.

The bloodhounds of the mighty,
The lawless men of the law,
Habeas Corpus, that the ones
Who had their freedom snatched,   370
May have their day in court.

Behold the bloodied river,
Like sheep led to the slaughter,
They were matched at dawn to the kill zone.

The accuser prosecuted and judged them
Unfit to remain inhabitants of the earth,
Ratatat! There was agony in their voice,
The last wails were the call for mothers,
for wives, sisters, and brothers,
Relatives sent to fetch ransom money   380
to pay enforcers of the law,
Enforcers turned murderers and kidnappers,
Habeas Corpus! **Ezu River** regurgitated its content,
The fishes were sated and the crimsoned river
Gave up its swollen tragedy as a spectacle
To a people who can be shocked no more.
"Do we exist to rain destruction on our brethren?
Had this thought of a union of the pen and the
bullet,

Thought that pen and the bullet could unite   390
to bring freedom,
It was at the final hours of death,
That I knew how wrong I was.

Dear ghoulish friend,
It was my assumption that those who are about
to die
Got some sort of warning when the throes of
Death arrived,
But for me, none of that occurred,
Instead, it was the agony of watching life   400
ebb out in rivulets,
The pain of watching stymied dreams,
The tears of the fizzling out of promises unfulfilled."

Dear netherworld reporter,
Yours was not the first act in the theatre of the
absurd,
Neither was it the first scene in the vaudeville of
calamity,
Tragedy is the first draft of history,
At the second, a segue into burlesque.   410

Thirty years you were gone,
While you walked and talked,
Power and its bloodhounds
Had the people in their gunsights,
The freedom of the individuals,
Anathema to the earthly potentates,

Hatred, fear, and tears were driven into the children
of men.

Babel was constructed in the absence of the
tower,   420
Confusion was sown amidst brothers of
men.
The restless, the young and the hopeless,
Target practices for licensed gunslingers.
"In my time, accidental discharge it was called."

Dear friend, what was accidental had become
brazen.

Putrefaction from early graves reached digital
amphitheatres,
New community congealed around hatred   430
for
Bloodshed by licensed gunslingers.

Like the bored panther,
Power initially played with its prey,
This new community mistook inaction for weakness,
Hence the digital alleys were left for the street
junctions,
The junctions where *Eshu* of Duality received
sacrifice,
They gathered in fellowship,   440
They gathered in unison,
They gathered to sing,
They honored the departed heroes

Who were felled by licensed projectiles,
At the flowering of the youth.

They begged for cessation of war declared by the
powerful
Against the crime of being weak and humble.
The singing and dancing crescendoed,
And the attendance grew daily like the   450
market for new yam.

The numbers grew and power pranced,
The first tool was babel without a tower,
For this, plebeian wolves were unleashed,
But unity and love increased the shrill cry for
cessation of killings,
The patience of Power reached the summit,
The encirclement of the prey is over,
Thus, at the word of the emperor,
Hell was unleashed on the children of hope,   460
The children who remembered not how
you,
Dear reporter, were sent away at the moment of
your bloom,
To the world where there is no return.

JOURNALIST KAY:

The Summer of silence have I seen,
It turned life into one long body trap,
A trap that forbade thought and speech,
This trap could be arrogant and uncouth,

And it could be camouflaged and   470
serpentine,
Different appearances with similar effects.
Once upon a time, I serenaded General
Khakistocracy,
The naivety of the pen in bed with bullets bubbled
like casked burgundy,
In retrospect, evil achieved consensual rape,
And for this, it achieved genius in the hall of
chicanery.
Can peace flow from the barrel of guns?   480
How foolish to expect debate in a hall of
veiled bayonets,
I gave up sight for swagger stick,
The General was naked, and I gave him the
borrowed tunic.
At the advent of the death of innocence,
The demise of fellowship was announced,
And freedom of speech remained the sole figure on
the cross of shame.

PART III

They showed up at the devil's dinner,
Devil's dinner, strictly by invitation,
Armed with long spoons, they arrived,
Sit far from the devil on the aisle-long table,
Take the choicest of meats, daintily nibble.

Like the pied piper, the devil charmed all,
Chianti in the decanters, Bordeaux of the deep past
From hilltop cellars in fluted grace passed around
by liveried hands,
No sin is as great as vanity, no dagger is as   10
sharp as charm,
Serenading minstrelsy, the best from the wretched
of the earth,
Or the despicable other, the stabilizing abyss.

They showed up at the devil's dinner.

The benevolence of the homestead
Compensates better than the life of a courtier,
"Away with your jaded philosophy!"
"The rich invited you to his party and you
declined?   20
When will your day arrive Mr. Hard-
Principle?"
"Tattered wisdom, even the fool knows that
There are no sunsets in the palace of the king,
And without reflection, it is settled that service to
The king is the service to the nation."
This matter, it shall have consequences,
 He that uses bare hands to draw fire,
Shall be rewarded with epileptic digits,
This matter shall have consequences.

"Nothing but fear stops the free-born from
Contesting for the vacant agnatic   30
chieftaincy."

CHORUS:

Keep dancing we've got your back,
Keep dancing we've got your back,
Dance to wherever you want,
Dance to wherever you like,
Keep dancing we've got your back!

Devil's dinners are lavish but seldom free,
But without foolishness wisdom has no value,
"We shall go, you are the one we shall meet,
"When returning from the mountains   40
delectable"

Ogun possessed water at home but chose blood
for birth,
The warrior prepares for battle,
But deity let it not be divulged by my mouth.

Dear mother why put the innocent in harm's way?
For the sake of the children's adulthood,
Ancient mothers attended the meetings of the avian.

You have eyes but you are blind,
You have a nose but smell not the   50
putrefaction,
Oh, happy children! Who brought you here today?
Who brought you to the citadel of blood and bones?
The king has gotten the throne the second time,

The road to the palace is paved with the bones of the
slaves,
The child of the deity shall not be sacrificed to the
deity,
But it is the child of the stranger that we
send on a   60
Journey of midnight return or the sojourn
to never come back,
Oh, happy children! Who brought you here this day?
"Dear friend of the Princess,
I shall not join in the procession,
Let you and your children walk with the damsels to
the palace,
I wait and tarry as my bowels need emptiness,
My apparels of nobility shall be sent ahead of me."

I shall tarry with the princess,   70
I shall wait for her highness,
Let the children go with the ladies-in-waiting,
Let them go with the guards to the palace,
The princess shall have the company of a friend.

Children of innocence!

Innocence of children,
Many lizards crawl but who knows the one with
stomach pains?
Nameless and invisible to power,
But known and valuable to their kin,   80
The land shed tears but unmeasured were
their steps,

The land is pregnant, but they paid no heed to its
protrusion,
Indeed, no unlucky head announces its presence
with a lump.

The king has gotten the throne the second time but
Hostilities had shifted the venue to the moment of
the gala,
It has been decided that victory song shall   90
become soulful dirge,
It has been decided that flutes for cocktails shall be
filled with raindrops of tears,
It has been decided that the happy procession shall
become cortege
And condolences shall be registered in the stead of
felicitations.

The apparition-masquerade chose nocturnal visits
to conceal its humanity.

That the gazelle might be caught at the   100
moment of rest
Made the panther ambush the watering holes before
daybreak.

The procession arrived without the princess,
The ambuscade knew not, fingers went to the
triggers,
And the Iron-god had his bath in the puddle of new
blood.

CHORUS:

Keep on dancing we've got your back,
Keep on dancing we've got your back,   110
Dance to wherever you want,
Dance to wherever you like,
Keep on dancing we've got your back!

Your epitaph is beautiful dear chief the honorable,
But you refused to sleep this early underworld morn,
"No bouquet, the flowers have ceased coming"
"The presence of the starry blue of plumbago,
Or the windy whites of the anemone,
Life is brief, fading like a sun-drenched   120
fresco."
Where are the lies in your truth oh departed jurist?
How I wish you lived the truth when you walked
upon the hill of sands.

At the devil's dinner, your ladle was long,
The plan was to eat the meal and chorister with the
angels,
Hence your equidistance between conscience and
oppression,
"But you know-"   130
The story is well known already!
To spite your friends, you became the devil's
advocate,
The devil never needed an attorney, but you were
charmed

with the preferment; finally, your talents and skills,
beckoned to be availed towards national service.

The ovation was loud, and the applause was long,
Philosophizing for bandits who have
cornered lucre?   140
You chose to believe the sculpted relief of
your imagination,
They wanted your gold to burnish their wood,
That the assembled congregants may genuflect
to the devil when they see an angel at his side,
You believed their lie of ceded power
And you made obeisance to the destroyer.

CHORUS:

Keep on dancing we've got your back,
Keep on dancing we've got your back,
Dance to wherever you want,   150
Dance to wherever you like,
Keep on dancing we've got your back!

The flowers, freshly cut carnations,
They stopped arriving because memories
Of the night of long knives faded from the offspring.
At mid-course, leave was taken from the table of
dainty,
It's time to return to the courts of the unyielding
angels.

Plans sinister choked the air like dark soot,   160

Intuition is the medication of the elders,
The string lacked intuition, it fell into the fire,
The plafond lacked intuition, it caved in,
The house-owner lacked intuition,
Got a visitation by the robbers,
The enemy reclines in the backyard,
But the betrayer is inside, sitting on the sofa.

Exited the devil's dinner in a loaned chariot,
The moment of the ambush is known to the
page.   170
The city of the angels must be barred
From its reprobate apostate.

The chariot lurched, the page grinned,
The gates of hades were flung open to the advocate
of the beast.

PART IV

"I am the duke, and he is the usurper!"

 owhere on earth is found power-beggars
Possessed of missionary zeal in the quest
To sit on the throne of the duchy.

Netherworld fool! The graveyard is
Filled with stymied idealists' bones.

Dear frustrated dukedom contender,

I do not serenade the restless dead,
But I give befitting second funeral.

Unhappy is the utopian who desired the   10
throne,
The throne of the fence-sitters' duchy,
The fence-sitters' duchy in the kingdom of recycled
miscreants.

"The homestead favours me" is the refrain of the
wise
To the entrapment by the wicked called coronet.

The hunters learned to shoot and the elephant
Made friends with elusion.

The elephant left the stretch of the   20
savannah,
And found habitation in the depths of the dark
forest.

The arrival of the elephant, a village can be fed.

The elephant journeyed far away from the citadel of
men.

Who shall bring back the elephant?
Who shall make a feast of it for the clan?
"I am the Tortoise, and I shall bring you the
elephant."   30

"But you shall give me its tusk and make me a titled chief"
The Tortoise journeyed to the depths of the forest,
The Tortoise crossed seven hills and seven rivers,
The Tortoise crossed seven valleys and seven fields,
The Tortoise found the elephant in the depths of the forest.

"Oh Tortoise, what brings you to my home?"
"*Kabiyesi ooooooo*![8] Your royal majesty!"   40
"Let the prank cease Tortoise! I am no king,
And the lineage of the elephants does not wear beaded crowns"
"No, your magnitude, the oracle has found you worthy,
This oracle is not cryptic like Delphi,
It clearly spoke the words of the gods,
It said, "the elephant or chaos",
And for this reason, the whole village bade me   50
To come to bring your royal immenseness to the throne,
To the throne of your fathers!"
"Silence Tortoise! I will stamp on you now"
"*Kabiyesi*, it is the sender of the message I fear and not the receiver,
The gods have appointed me to deliver their words and I shall do it,

---

[8] A salutation made to Yoruba kings by their subjects.

Oh King Elephant! Oh mighty elephant,
See the garlands of honour on your   60
magnificent body,
See the turquoise beads of authority on your neck,
Kabiyesi Elephant, step forward your majesty,

HEAR WHAT THE TOWN SAID:

"We'll make the Elephant King, ***Eweku-elele***!
"We'll make the Elephant King, ***Eweku-elele***!
Oh King Elephant! The stretch of the body
economizes flowing raiment,
Oh King Elephant! Jaded eyes and easy steps
of royalty!
Kabiyesi Elephant! The one a woman met   70
on the road
And collapsed into tears and wailed,
"Dear me, Dear me,
How I wish this is one's husband or one's adulterer"
Dear Tortoise stop the adulations,
So, it is true I am a King? I knew that I am royalty.

Kabiyesi Elephant, leave the wilderness,
The palace beckons,
The head that is fit for the crown does not
sleep in the open,   80
The palace and the throne is waiting for
your highness.

"I shall follow you Tortoise; I shall follow you"
They crossed seven rivers and seven mountains,

They crossed seven valleys and seven fields.

"Tortoise, I return to my place,
The throne is no good for me,
My honesty is poison for politics,
Tortoise, let me return now."

"We'll make Elephant King, **Eweku-elele**!"　　90
"We'll make Elephant King, **Eweku-elele**!"
Kabiyesi Elephant, "**Ajanaku** I saw a darting movement"
Let us stop envy and declare that we have seen
the mighty Elephant!

Your honesty is the recipe for our progress,
"We'll make the Elephant King, *Eweku-elele*!"
"We'll make the Elephant King, *Eweku-elele*!"
Dear Tortoise, your words are like
sweetened bean cakes.　　100

The throne stood on carpeted earth,
The town made obeisance to the Elephant,
Royal drums heralded the arrival of the choice
of the oracle.

Death sought to entrap the cunning,
The cunning sought to entrap death.

Danger lurks in the farm of **Longẹ**,
Indeed, **Longẹ** himself is dangerous.
"We'll make Elephant King, *Eweku-elele*!"

"We'll make Elephant King, *Eweku-elele*!"   110
People of New Era city!
If many riders ride inside my belly,
They shall find a paved road and will not stumble,
For my happiness is of no limits.

When my good friend Tortoise brought the good
tidings,
My credulity vanished,
But I have seen today that I am to become the
King of New Era,
For this I promise you that a new era has   120
begun in New Era.

"We'll make the Elephant King, *Eweku-elele*!"
"We'll make the Elephant King, *Eweku-elele*!"
Thank You, Thank You! Let me step to my throne,
Let me become, truly, your majestic king.

Two steps forward, the ground shifted under the
Elephant,
The carpet gave way and the once concealed large
ditch was uncovered,
Epiphany arrived at the moment when the   130
Elephant's bulk hit the bottom of the abyss.

And the town brought out spears, daggers, and
swords.

The elephant's meat is best enjoyed when
tenderized.

Dear friend, death waits for all with a question,
You have answered yours; we shall answer ours.
The one who fell into a ditch,
Teaches the laggards valuable lessons on
the nature of the road.   140

You were dispatched to the bank of the Styx
By those who found your living meddlesome.

The Duchy of Fence-sitters,
Where citizens call for light but preferred it deemed,
Where darkness is hated but regularly kept in
employment.

The Duchy of Fence-sitters,
Where they danced behind heroes and elected
villains to the dukedom,
"Keep dancing, we've got your back," they   150
tell their champions,
But when tribulations arrive, they pitch tents with
their oppressors.

The Duchy of Fence-sitters,
Where the best dukes are the ones that never ruled,
Where the greatest rulers ruled from their epitaphs.
The Duchy of Fence-sitters,
Time is frozen for the geriatrics
And adults are perpetual children.

If you catch up with him, kill him.   160

If he outruns you, scoop his footprints.

The town's vagabond is the one beloved by all men,
The marketplace buffoon is the joy of onlookers.
Leader of Opposition! Duke-in-waiting,
Serfdom was veneered with democracy,
There is freedom before the speech but seldom after.

Mean men who gave edicts and never dialogue,
They wanted dynasties and not elections.
Rulership forever! Unquestionable
potentates   170
Accountable to none;
They are the early mourners at the
House of the ones they murdered.

All lizards are prostrating but the one with stomach
pains is unidentifiable.

Autopsy: middle-aged male,
Cause of death: strangulation.

'Tis from the distance, the one with sunken eyes,
'Tis from the distance he must start wailing.

It approaches; we must set trap for it.   180
Opposition becomes the conscience of the
society-unacceptable!

Voices had been siloed and the serfs had been
marooned,

Lies repeated more than Goebbels' and they became truths.

Strangulate consciousness,
Bring back lullaby,
And return them to sleep.

THE ARCHAEOLOGY

Dear ***Olokun***, it's time to give up your dead,
Let those who chose freedom in the belly
Of the ocean speak or remain silent forever.

Olokun, you were propitiated by those
Who made others weep for their own laughter,
For this reason, you are the willing accomplice
In the four-hundred-year darkness,
The darkness which forged heaven,
Heaven made from the gnashing of teeth,
From the serration of meaty flesh   10
By cowhide whips which sweetened tea-
time sugar.

Olokun you are the crime, the vilest of them all!
Therefore, let the dead speak this windy morn,
For it is their reasonable service.

PART I

That I may hear the inaudible, I plucked the
auditory leaves,
That I may see the invisible, I dipped eyes in the
tears of heavenly smith,
That I may recall, I ingested the serum of   20
consciousness
Poseidon or *Olokun*, you must give up
The dead you chained in your dark belly,
For the time of unearthing has arrived.

And the orphaned truth must find a home.

Seven manilas, seven cowries, and seven
tortoiseshells,
the sacrifice at the banks of the ancient gates of hell,
Elmina, Bunce Island or Goree[9],
Wherever and all over,   30
Accept the Offertory, abominable *Olokun*
And give up your secrets in peace.

You were the accomplice,
The Judas of compromise.
Who threw curtains of darkness?
On the face of the hapless ones who left delicacies
for your little ones.

---

[9] Names of the Castles built by the Portuguese [Elmina in Ghana], the English[Bunce
Island in Sierra Leone], and the French [Goree at Senegal] for processing and
preparing slaves for shipment to the Americas.

Ekaabo and *Akwaaba*, the unity of welcome,
For *Akosua* and *Aduke* at the astern of
hell,   40
Chaperoned by *Olokun* who brought wealth
To those who kept their brethren in lightless coops,
That they may toil for the payment for further
oppression,
The guns of oppression, the cowries of tears
Or the horses of tribulation.
Akosua lend me your eyes for the vision is foggy,
Once the child's eyes are blown, the clearer they see.
Similarities of colour, the sameness of trauma.

But barricaded by tongue and all resorted to   50
wailing,
Even the deaf can talk and for this, the hands found
the words.

Birth pangs in the bowels of the Hades' Voyager?
The eyes of babes deserved goodness,
But the arrival at the feet of manacled father,
The chattering in unison of violated maids,
A leg in the stock and the mother in stoic,
Peeled skinned jailer's entry into the hold,
Arrival in time when mother deranged   60
Sent the young soul to the place of the
shadows.

"Wait not for me oh child of faceless seeds!"
Umbilical cord for a chokehold,

New birth and after birth, dumped inside the sacks
of coldness.

Calm seas and happy winds,
Tonic Gin Ale for the mates,
And dark rum, good Cap'n Phillips,
The lemon for scurvy and the ale for good   70
company.

SING NOW THE 'OLE SAILORS OF GUINEA' SONG:

Guinea calls for the Bristol-men,
Promised tusks and the negro's arms
For the sugar and rum we care,
And the tales of happy is told.
Noonday till all is gone,
We've got nothing but dreams and more,
My friend the morn has come,
When teeth are filled with gold.

Akosua, Aduke, Ngiza,
Drunken sailors have no oil for stormy seas   10
on a sedate night,
Except for that which raged in the loins.

Vacant eyes met libidinous desires,
The body is the witness to its plunder,
The soul, already sent flying across the ocean
But never reaching home,
The home and hearth forever wasted,

And the soul returned when pigs grunted satiation,
And the maidens' feet returned into the
firm clasp of Iron.   20

Akosua the betrothed,
Akosua, the mutilation of the spirit,
Angst is no cure for despondency,
The land embraced aridity in the stead of death,
But for a man, death is faster than ignominy.

Let death find us and bring our spirits to the
hunting grounds of our ancestors.

Fool! Even death is not available for choice,
Condemned here to sit out tribulations in
iron-clad melancholy.   30

For those who found choice in death,
Let those ones seek company with me,
For eventide arrive when they come for the fair
Akosua and others,
And the unlatched hold is the time,
The time to find escape in ages-long sleep.

Guinea calls for the Indies-men,
Promised tusks and the negro's arms
For the sugar and rum we care,
And the tales of happy is told.   40

Noonday till all is gone,
We've got nothing but dreams and more,

My friend the morn has come,
When teeth are filled with gold.

The time has arrived and freedom calls,
The cat's hind does not kiss the earth,
When the storm charges, it sidesteps the water
deity,
The Rhinoceros holds no confab with the
fox due to age difference,   50
All yokes of Iron have no meaning for the
one who shared a gourd with the Iron-god,
I am the one who broke free from the forge even
with chains,
No matter the entrapment of the snake, it finds a
crack and slides through,
Today I slide through and shall no longer be
repressed!

They wanted to know the reasons for the
chatter in the yard,   60
I told them it is the Iron-deity I swallowed,
Hence the invincibility of the mill.

There is a fearsome deity in the junction house,
'Tis daily it drinks red oil,
This deity is the transformer of wood to a living
being,
And a living being to a lifeless wood.
The projectile that is true to the coconut tree
Cannot drink the hidden liquid of the
unshelled nuts,   70

And the wind's fury is not enough to empty the
coconut of its sealed water,
I entered the catacombs of existence to eat with the
owners of life,
I entered the coven and I supped with the bearded
female elders,
The broken gourd is pregnant with meaning,
A meaning that can only be unraveled by the
collision of meteors,
Thus, when elements collide one must   80
bend,
Chains have collided with the furnace today and it
must become magma!

The aft deck, sound the alarm!
Bedlam in slave's hold!
Unchained, unfastened, and unlatched!
Gather the muskets and let wounds bring restrain!
Spare even the recalcitrant,
For their life is the treasure.

Akosua come with me,   90
The place of long shadows calls.

For swifter is death than ignominy,
And beyond this passage is a garden made for love.

The boom of muskets, the ricochet of iron
Black heads severed by scimitars grabbed by hasty
white hands,
But nothing shall stop the sons of free lords

From the warm embrace of death.

Willing bodies was heaved,
The green waves laughed,   100
Akosua, Nana, more names forever lost,
And living bodies hit the chilled ocean.

PART II

We become effigies when we embrace death.
Irrespective of the number of times the soul
Of the hornbill is summoned,
Its thousand-year lifetime destiny is assured.

You have journeyed from the other side of
the seas of strife,
Through Saccharum reeds, you made the
journey home,
On arrival, you refused to enter the house,   10
Standing akimbo upon oceanic
perturbations,
Why refuse to make entry?

REPLY:

Ours is the testament written in blood cauldrons.
That it may not be said that men walked meekly
To their chains and manumission came by the
Generous grace of those who questioned
The mandate of the heavens and mastered the
world,
We transformed existence and set our souls   20
Free from bodied cubicles and sought union
With the ancestors in the sacred groves of Africa.
Indeed, the earth is the place of commerce,
If captured and sold like common wares of

Ejigbomekun market, peace was found in the
Thought of being gathered with the ancestors
When we bowed to accept the shroud.
Blackness was the crime,
Imprisonment for life, the term.
We drank bitterness for other's sweetness,   30
Daylong toils for other's leisure,
Our salty sweats, their sweetened rest,
Lacerating whiplash to rouse the drowsy,
Sunlight met with hidden tears.

The rainbow serpents the sky in a spectrum
The light is one, but **Olodumare** made the prism,
That human may come in yellow, pink, brown,
Sepia, red, olive, hues, and shades of one light at
dawn.

'Humankind is one among many' we say,   40
'Man is the king of all they said.

'We are all humans' we say.

'Maybe in the past but not in the present' they say.

In the days gone by, the head cannot be shaved in
the absence of the head-owner,
But their court sat and sent us to the bare life in
absentia,
He-men before the arrival of Eternia,
The masters of the Universium,

Declared from Olympus the encyclical of the damned:

Sin is blackness and blackness, the bare life,   50
Sacred for toil and unacceptable in death to
the gods.

Part III

SANS SOUCI

The hills of Milot have kept silent,
Silent sentinels and willing accomplices
To the murder of that which was dead.

But silent hills shall be roused from unearned sleep,
Even the murdered ghosts shall be made to talk.
Sans Souci the palace of Henry[10],
Henry the one without peer
In the annals of chicanery,
Sans Souci you are the fraud!

Your ruins bear the testimony,   10
And your tattered ermine gave you away!

Sans Souci, the soil of Milot shuddered
At the toil of the free exerted on you,
For this reason, many quakes wasted you,
That in the lie, that you may deceive others not.

---

[10] Henry Christophe, One of the leaders of the Haitian Revolution. He ordered the assassination of one of the leaders of the insurgents who never surrendered to France in the early years of the Revolution, Colonel Jean-Baptiste Sans-Souci. He also ordered the killing of the Hero of the Battle of Vertieres, Brigadier Francois Capoix 'La Mort'. He made himself king of the half part of Saint Domingue Island and he put his newly freed people to forced labour so as to build the King's Palace at Milot. He named the Palace Sans Souci so that the world would forget the Sans-Souci the Revolutionary.

But posterity cared not for silenced ghosts,
Or for the entreaties of manacled apparitions.

Sans Souci you are ruined and the journey to Milot
Is not for your picturesque value,
Or for the retelling of the story of the ego it   20
failed to mask.

Sans Souci the ruin must give up Sans Souci the
Man,
For even bayoneted ghosts deserve their salve.

REPLY:

Many visited and many arrived,
Come one and come all,
The ruined wonder of the black world beckoned,
Heaven's gate is firmly locked,
Hence, I became the tour guide
And told the world what it wanted to hear.   30

AGBONMIREGUN:

Mon Colonel, Mon Colonel,
This ear is deaf to worldly musicals,
If history shall not accept you into its fold,
You are invited to come into the Apocrypha,
The orphaned tomes in the chthonic crypts.
If the canons rejected you,
And said that Prometheus cannot be black,

And light cannot be brought out from the one
marooned in darkness,
Then it is time that you seek company in   40
the library of the rejected!

REPLY:

Who is the man that sought liberty?
That he may have no cares in the world?
I, Jean-Baptiste Sans Souci,
The first and the last of my name,
Akanga in the old country,
But care-free on the battlefield.

The tale that you sought,
Is the tale whose dawn is in Bakongo[11],
Whose noon is in the mountains of   50
Hispaniola,
And whose night is in the ruins of Milot.

But if this tale shall find a place in the library of
rejected,
Then it shall be told for writing pleasure
And the ghouls who cherish the tales
Of curmudgeon ghosts shall find ecstasy.

The canopies of the Kongo jungle hid the seething
vendetta
From the gaze of the cumulus-tinged skies,   60

---

[11] Native name for the present-day Congo country.

Brothers drank the poisoned chalice
And drew a sword on each other,
Inside war, I was born,
Inside war, I grew
And inside war, I was nurtured.

Men became money and brothers pillaged brothers,
That easy lucre can be found,
The white enemies found Luanda
But brothers foraged the jungle for the
living gold,   70
That the debt of oppression can be paid
with a surplus of tears.

Akanga's unsandaled feet ran through briars and
thorns,
It became a fugitive to save the life he knew,
The life of freedom and nothing more.

The puppets are black but white hands pulled the
strings,
But the foliage of the jungle hid both the
string and the puppeteer,   80
Akanga swam faster than the crocs through
rivers,
Akanga calloused hands gripped blade,
It slashed both vines and men,
Men who netted men for wealth.

One morn when sleep stiffened the bones,
And locked the eyes when the body found

Comfort in the creviced bedding,
Brothers of man arrived,
But not with good tidings.   90

Sleep vanished but the net was faster.

The feet were shackled and the hands which
Fought were bound in chains.

This was the end of Akanga.

AGBONMIREGUN:

Akanga died that Sans Souci may be birthed.

The arrival of chains does not kill the man,
But the acceptance of silence in the face of tyranny.

REPLY:

If ghosts were allowed a chuckle,
A guffaw would have accompanied it.

'Tis true Akanga never died,   100
But Akanga was muzzled, not in life but in
death,
He was muzzled, that it may not be known that a
redeemer can also be black.

The body yields only to a willing spirit,
And enslavement comes only to the
compromised soul,

This spirit made a covenant with freedom,
Chains are not the accoutrements of piety,
Nor shackles, the symbol of princely rank.   110

Like dirty money, many times in many
hands,
Passed from one to another.

The paths widened and the forests receded,
Criminals with no convictions,
Starved and naked and marched to the coasts,
And black hands gave living gold to white hands,
Au revoir! Adieu l'Afrique!
Clement winds pushed the sails,
And the willing sea carried the wooden jail.   120

Many times, death visited,
He conversed with me inside the jail at sea,
But I have made a covenant with liberty.

The warrior's back is stiff and knows no king,
Even death has no bribes for the one who
fought to live!

Death took some and others flung their bodies to
The embrace of death,
For all who died on the watery road to hell,
Theirs was the unrivaled bravery.   130

The gold must be living for its value in
exchanges,

If the gold is dead, it becomes carrion for vultures,
Or food for fishes that have canines,
And ruin for those whose limited liability is the
venture of the ocean.

As for those who chose life in chains,
Complicity with captors was not the goal,
'That we may relay freedom to posterity,
We kept death in abeyance till the day after   140
the morrow."

But like the scales of onion,
The morrow has many layers,
Opening to new folds at new dawns,
Tempting the living with new lies called hope,
That the masters of the world may be sated with
the lie
That the tillers of the earth shall forever be
wretched,
And those who are bound to the toil shall   150
have new expectations of freedom.

The Sea-jail anchored and living golds found
terra firma.

Few days at the sea-side piazzas,
Fresh off the boat, new living gold,
Minted coins for a living currency,
Bill of sale to the master of man-property,
And the bundle of the natural life of blackness,
The profits of a tomorrow of laughter built

On the sweats, pain, and tears of those sent   160
out of common humanity,
So that the location of their hell near the
manicured paradise
And their late-night weeping shall not trouble
the sleep of those
Who used fellow men in the rituals of avarice
and lucre.

Akanga did not die but was locked away.
He was locked for another to emerge,
Another that will accept chains with the joy   170
of a dog,
Another that will daily mine gold from his brows,
back, and loins
And hand over wealth willingly to those who ruled
the world.

For this reason, the parson came,
'Old things must pass away and all things must
become new!'

'I baptize you in the name of the Father
Je te baptize au nom du père, et du fils, et   180
du saint esprit.

Old things have passed away,
Jean-Baptiste is the new, newly fitted for bondage.
Sugar-reeds and overseer's whip,
Dawn to dusk toiling till the hour of death,
And yet, liberty called.

Liberty called and sang into our ears,
But for our whispered memorials of liberty in
Kongo,
The ones born in chains called us   190
Bozzales[12],
Africans in chains.

If the Bozzales were once free,
Surely, they shall be free once more,
In life and not in death.

Their shouts and contestations
Pierced through the curtains of sugar,
It roused the somnambulist slaves,
And new words were picked by the
wretched of the fields,   200
Libertè, fraternitè, ègalitè[13],
White slaves beheaded their king and Queen,
And proclaimed all men free, all men brothers, and
all men equal.

White slaves are free, black slaves shall be free!
White lips smirked,
"Oh no! Who says you are men?"

---

[12] Name given to slaves in Haiti who were born in Africa. This is to differentiate them
from Creoles, who are slaves or freed blacks, or Mullatos that were born in Haiti. The
Bozzales were the ones under the leadership of Sans Souci and others who refused to
surrender to France and instead embarked on four-year Guerilla warfare against
France and other Creoles who initially surrendered to France during the Haitian
Revolution.
[13] The ideals of the French Revolution of 1789.

High in the mountains, we gathered,
Freedom is not only for the whites,
Boukman[14] talked and the spirits   210
were summoned:
Ours is the fate of liberty
Ours is the destiny of death!

We, who were sent out of the congregation of
mankind,
Shall find freedom for ourselves and our offspring,
The ancestors said two generations must not be
born in chains,
Alas! The memory of liberty has been wiped
from forty!   220

The gourd plant claimed the path with its
tentacles,
We take what has been destined for us,
When the lion still possesses its paws,
Unborn is the animal that wags tails on its
nostrils,
The thunder killed in hundreds,
They accused thunder of murder,
The thunder shrugged and declared itself
blameless,   230
Hence, when it killed,
'Oh thunder!' They exclaimed,

---

[14] Dutty Boukman, was one of the early leaders of the Haitian Revolution and Voodoo
Priest. He was later captured and hanged by the White slaveholders in Haiti.

When it wasted, they gave thanks to the father of
destruction,
When the thunder-god revolts in the heavens,
Earthlings run helter-skelter to find cover,
The hour of wrath has finally arrived!
When the terra-cotta effigy desires shame,
It asks for a river-side ablution.

The egret owned all shades of white,   240
Thus, where the egret settles to wash its
apparel,
The partridge dares not make a showing.
We have arrived, let the whole forest make
habitation with frightened silence!

Slumber vanished and the eyes became clear,
Masters dialogued with legs and found speed,
Slaves broke their chains and filed behind standards
of liberty.

Freedom is a sour grape,   250
Those who are thirsty have no throats that
say no.

But for some among us, who found sweet wine in
the cellars of the jailers,
And the promises of the peerage in the realm of the
enslavers,
Freedom for the brethren, a meal of convenience.
Bayonets and terror failed,

And Empire brought wiles and charms into
service,   260
Louverture, Christophe, Dessalines,
Pétion[15],
Empire became coquettish and called you generals,
Ermined devils saluted you and you sheathed your
swords,
Mes Généraux ! The standards of the enemy sway
aloft,
Black banners, tattered and flying still,
Forward to the death! *Vive la revolution*!

LOUVERTURE:

Colonel Jean-Baptiste Sans Souci!   270
You must obey the last order of your
General,
The revolution is over *pour le moment*,
You shall stand down and await further instructions,
Ours is freedom amid empire,
The sceptre is ours and the scimitar in our grip,
The empire stretches arms for an embrace,
Like iniquitous children we accept.

The empire calls for fellowship,
It's time to take what is given,   280
For the arms are nearing exhaustion
And the blades have reached bluntness.

---

[15] Toussaint Louverture , Henry Christophe, Jean-Jacques Dessalines, Alexandre
Petion.

Now Colonel! Stand Down!

Mon cher Général,
Liberty or death is the standard of the revolution,
You are a man of this world,
I am a man of the old world,
The old world of the canopied forests,
And jagged-edge mounts,
The place where dusty paths are eaten by   290
unsandalled feet,
Where mothers glisten ebony skins with camwood
tears,
In the old world, death is embraced faster than
ignominy.

Liberty or death is the standard of freedom,
For the cause of freedom, I become renegade,
Renegade to the whites, renegade to the blacks,
To the blacks who sought friendship with
the hands   300
Which spilled black blood for cooked sugar.

For me and freedom, an oath has bound:

Till death do us part.

I, Jean-Baptiste Sans Souci,
The first of the brethren who sought glory in death,
Fire for fire, iron for iron, blood for blood,
Freedom is seldom served *a la carte*

The stockings of the rooster must be removed with
fire.

It shall go with it,   310
The vine that grips the elephant on its way
to the river,
It shall go with it!
We are the boas, and no pocket of man can
contain us.

Let those who sought the vengeance of Golgotha,
Let those who broke chains with bleached skulls
of the lashers,
Come with me!

The course of liberty shall be pursued to the   320
end of the earth,
Montagne Noire, Black Mountains opened its
bowels,
Its foliaged canopies meshed with our slave fatigues,
The heavens quenched our thirsts,
And the beads of dews on the verdant filled our
flasks.
Wild apples for dinner, bitter herbs for serum,
Hunch-back squirrels for lunch,
Smoked venison for dinner,   330
From caves to crevices we marched,
And raised the standards of liberty up high.

Where men walked, trees moved with them,

For the sake of freedom, we entered oath with the
earth,
That those who betrayed the earth shall be
swallowed in its core,
We stood upon the earth, we ate the bush rat,
We stood upon the earth, we ate the flying
fowl,   340
The earth gave the word, we cease to die.

They have their way, we have ours,
Theirs is to roll many drums,
And form long columns,
Many colours, chevalier and epaulettes,
Swift charges of horsemen,
Testudo, barricades, fusillades,
And the fury of hell from the blast of angry canons.
Who engages a juggernaut with axes and
glory?   350

Only the fool! Only the suiciding martyr!
But the cause of freedom is best served by the living,
And the tree of liberty is best watered with the blood
of the enemy!

The horse is fair-natured
But men gave it venom.

We traded space for time,
We allowed the lion to hunt the prey,
But for the lion to savour its meal, it found
no rest,   360

For we are the winged- hyenas,
We swooped in unison and laughed in staccato,
Intrigue against the stone mill cannot be done
While standing upon the stone mill,
We communed with the ancestors
And used red oil to eat *kola*[16],
We became fortified
And boomeranged enchantment to the enchanter.

Yet, fortification owns the day of
catastrophe,   370
But the soul-deity owns the day of
redemption.

Was a mere stripling when the words
Of the oracle coursed through my mouth,
Was between child and man
When the secrets of the elders were kept with me.
The bat faced downwards, and nothing escaped its
view.

From the summits of Massif du Nord[17],
Like the primates of the skies,   380
We leaped on Massif de la Hotte.[18]
The enemy wanted the fight,

---

[16] Kola-nut. When combined with red oil in consumption, it becomes the Equivalent of the Holy Eucharist.

[17] A mountain in Haiti.

[18] A mountain in Haiti.

But we had all the time.

When he charged, we moved.
When he was weary, we charged.

We conspired with the forests,
We became the initiates of the chameleon,
And adorned the fatigues of our surroundings.
They came in liveried blues,
We came like moving trees.   390

We howled with our fusillades,
And before the truth of our bullets,
The enemy staggered in many deaths!

'Twas at the moment when the enemy rejoiced my
plight,
That he fell, to be fastened in a shroud.

I asked what killed the evil one,
They said it was two ruinations that visited him,
I asked what shackled him,
They said it was the pestilence king who   400
shackled him.

They told me to proceed to the place of the coven,
I replied that it was the bearded mothers,
Who took me to the higher grounds.

War invaded me in the forests,
I became the lord of the forests.

Those who summoned our souls for evil,
Shall avail their heads for the consequences
of their curses.
The pigeon does not flap wings and   410
becomes entrapped,
Instead, it takes to the skies, away from the
slingshot of the prowler.

Victory is complete and the Empire recedes.
But the black generals who once bowed to
conspiracy,
Now garlanded with laud.

AGBONMIREGUN:

With your band, you roamed the mountains,
Like the lone leopard, you embraced the
nights,   420
And in the morning, you clutched victory.
But you died and vanished from history.
Who killed the lion of the mountains?
Who exorcised the ghost of the victor?
And killed him the first and the second time?

It is the fate of the black savior to be felled by
friendly bullets.

From the mountains, I was summoned,
Henry Christophe dropped the general's
epaulettes for the crown.   430

Liberty has been won and swords must become
ploughshares,
'Let's have a tete-a-tete, we are first brothers
And then comrades' said, Henry.

The dinner charmed the soul thirsty for fineries,
But the way of man is a permanent state of war,
For this, I announced my departure mid-course,
The hand must not tarry in the hole of the scorpion,
An extended stay at the place of defecation
invites the companies of flies.   440

But who comes to dinner party with
daggers?
If not the traitorous?

Who hides pistols behind wine-flutes?
If not the traitorous?

The horses have bolted,
Grinning black faces announced the arrival of death,
Humans! Stinger of the child with the mother!

I know poison and I know danger,
But I failed to see chicanery and brewing   450
intrigue.
Boom! Boom! And the Colonel fell in the company
of friends.

AGBONMIREGUN:

It's time to rest dear Colonel,
You fought for black eternity,
And snatched victory from the jaws of hell.

Find rest and roam no more.

For if history shall not have a place for you in the
canons,
Yours shall be a shelf of prime,   460
In the library of the Apocrypha.

GOLGOTHA AT VERTIERES

Beneath the Empire is filth,
Filth! Blood! Bones! And sweat of the earth's
wretched.

Dessalines! Capoix la Mort!
Three centuries of bare life and assured death.

We have sworn fealty to freedom
And vowed allegiance to liberty,
We journeyed with the wind
And we made tempest our companion.

The day of redemption has arrived,   10
Salvation comes in many colours,
And today it is black.

Golgotha is Cap- Haitien,
All scores shall be settled.

The cup is full and the deluge of their shame,
The embankment it has torn.

If the heavens blinked, it is the flash of the lightning,
If the skies coughed, it is the boom of the thunder,
But if the black avengers go berserk, it is the
surge of freedom.   20

Fort Bréda, Fort Bréda,
The day of atonement has arrived.

Bunting of tyranny, the companion of the moats of-
'Find joy in others' tears'
Fort Bréda coughed smoke and bellowed dark
outrage,
Annoyance in the heavens,
Waste and tumult upon the earth!

'Forgive him, endure it' made-
The vulture to become bald.   30

They are the ones who introduced
The cobra to the guild of the venomous.

Vertières behind and Charrier ahead,
I, Capoix the Death, whose acquaintance dare not
meet,
And who was met by the carefree stranger.

Bucephalus neighed under Alexander,
François Capoix charged forward with liberty!

In the stead of death, land has chosen
aridity,   40

'Tis the runner who looks askance at the moving of the day.

Into the Ravine, towards Charrier,
Liberté ou la mort! We till the fields for others' belly no more.

Enemy's volley, angry fusillades, and colliding cannonballs.

We have made a covenant with destiny,
We shall forge freedom with the ink of blood
And write justice on the vellum of the   50
tyrants' carcass.

Ricocheting cannonballs,
Equestrian fall and a stallion in the throes of death,
Sabre clenched, journey on foot and I raised the standard high,
Liberté ou la mort! Liberté ou la mort!
Ours is the remission paid with blood,
The road to paradise is filled with thorns and briars,
But we stood to be counted among men,
And exit the cages and the coops,   60
Where sons of men have banished us.
Liberté ou la mort! Liberté ou la mort!
Sons of revolution! do not despair,
The road widened; the road opened.

Avance! Avance!
The Swallow built its nest in the skies –

while facing the central yard.
Death for death, blood for blood
Iron for iron and life for life.

We have run the distance, 70
We have reached the kindred of the fiends,
Let your hell meet their perditions.

Overhead the heavens erupted catastrophe,
At the flanks, barrages of fiery malice,
But we are the rage of the cornered dragon,
The pent-up fury of the desert viper.

Avance! Avance!
For liberty waits at the doorway of death,
Forward! Forward! For glory inhabits the
realms with pains. 80

Sons of liberty, charge with me!
Heaven recedes, for we postponed arrival,
We have become the offspring of the artful death-
dodger,
We die another day. *Avance! Avance!*

Settlement for today and never tomorrow,
Today is named today,
Because of the present called finalization.
Unacceptable! The tail of the lion, a
plaything of a hyena? 90
Avalanche of thunder overhead,
Flood of molten hell on the flanks,

But death has no power over zero,
And diseases have no single hold on the plains.

*A canon ball whizzed through the air and knocked
off the hat of General François Capoix. He picked
his hat and moved with his men forward.*

Capoix la mort, I am death!

They booked death for my case,
Death arrived, but it was postponement   100

sine die,
When tomorrow arrives,
Like layers of the onion, another morrow shall
unfold.

Vertiéres, Vertiéres,
Earthlings how is the ordeal on earth?
Denizens of hades, how is the agony?
War is not baked black-eyed peas,
War is not honey bread,
War is unlike the warming sleep with the   110
consort of delight.

The house contained it not,
The road is not wide enough,
But this road is open
And I shall enter.

Silence fell on the French Fort.

Lone equestrian cladded in the Empire's colours,
Descended the hills was swift gallops,
Dismounted and waved truce,
"General you have forged your name in   120
glory,
Your bravery in the face of death is unrivaled,
General Rochambeau sends his regards."

Mounted once more and galloped uphill to the
beleaguered fort.

The truce is over, drumbeats accompanied
bellowing canons,
Avance! Avance! Forward! Forward!

I, Jean-Jacques Dessalines,
The commander and the avenger of the   130
free,
My bulging eyes is the fury of the thunder god,
But this day have I set for the task of completion,
And here in Vertiéres, all debts shall be paid off.

The yard is the name that we call the dawn,
Penetrating gaze is the name of the noonday.

The gates of liberty have opened,
For the lineage of the canine does not pay a toll
at the entrance.

Rochambeau! The outside has no hiding   140
place for the sunlight,
The day has broken upon you.

Indeed, the dog that will undress the lion shall be
Birthed in its own blood.

We swam across the tempestuous seas
And we knew its mysteries.

You asked what the mystery is?
And I replied that it is the mystery of anguished
run amok.

We staggered in the arena where the mighty   150
fell,
We became the sons of death, and we are invincible.
We became the children of pestilence, we have
immunity.

Rochambeau! It is I Dessalines who calls you,
Saint Domingue is lost to you,
The jewel of France is gone forever.

ROCHAMBEAU:

Dessalines you believed your own lies.
Saint Domingue Francais!
Lay down your arms   160
and you shall receive pardon.

Lay down your arms!

DESSALINES:

The prickly Amaranth is not edible,
The thorny Amaranth is not palatable,
They ate the spinach and wanted to extend the same
courtesy
To the Amaranth?
The Amaranth cannot be eaten!
It shall be dragged with the Elephant,
It shall be pulled along with it,   170
The vine that decided to halt the Elephant
On its way to the Mountain of foe-crushing,
It shall be pulled along to its destruction.

Valour without discretion landed the ladle in a
boiling cauldron,
Unskillfulness in disobedience landed the poker
inside the furnace,
Like Leclerc[19], Saint Domingue shall bury you,
For it shall never be yours.
Liberté ou la mort![20]   180
Sons of freedom advance!
Here is the last stand against the despots,
The final sepulchre of the dominion of race,

---

[19] Charles Leclerc, French general, brother-in-law of Napoleon, who attempted to
suppress the Haitian revolt led by the former slave Toussaint Louverture.

[20] Liberty or Death! Haiti's Slogan during the Revolution.

The mausoleum of the humanity of bestiality.
We have become the fearsome,
We shall avenge the bloodied debts of history,
Sons of liberty swoop on the leash holders,
Trials or ruination?
Belch thunder! Shower hell,
For the hour of liberty has come.   190

The heavens opened and Cap-Haitien was
drenched in rain. Dessalines sent more
reinforcements to Brigadier François Capoix'
brigade. The white pennant of truce and surrender
could be seen on General Rochambeau's fort. The
war is over.

Rochambeau, you chose wisdom,
For fleeing is the antidote to a lost battle.
The weary fled, that the remnant of lives
May be preserved.   200

NOW HEAR THIS:

The grumbling grunts remained sealed within the
pig,
'Tis the exit of the projectile that we see
And never its boomerang,
Leave Saint Domingue now and never return,
Leave Saint Domingue! Leave now!

Here is the Testament of Vertières,
Tell it on the Kilimanjaro- Forward! Forward!

Tell it in the Sahara- Forward! Forward!
Tell it on the Niger- Forward! Forward!   210
Tell it in the Kalahari- Forward! Forward!
Tell it in the Caribbean- Forward! Forward!
Tell it to all the dispossessed- Forward! Forward!
General Francois Capoix "The death," says-
Forward! Forward!

THE JOURNEY TO NANDO

PART I

The pot crashed and the water emptied,
His wife and unborn child left for **Kh'indo**
at noon,
At the hour of birth when water mixed with blood,
They departed and the household women let out
dirges of bitterness.

'Tis four seasons since Chido[21] willed it,
'Tis four harvests of corn since Ama accepted the
bride of youth
The scar remained but the pain is gone,   10
And Shishi Atobe shall take a new wife.

You are my betrothed and I am your shield,
Ours is the union sanctioned by the gods,
From your hand, I shall drink new **burukutu,**

---

[21] Jukun's equivalent of the European conceptualization of God.

Burkutu from the millet and sorghum from the
fields,
From fields planted by my sinews and my brawn.
Your hands shall ladle porridge and scoop molten
beans,
And your bosom shall be my delight at   20
eventide.

The day has come, and the hour has arrived,
The rains arrived and the fields must be planted,
But the Lord of the corn must depart,
He must leave **Puje** and depart for **Nando**,
The day has come, and the moment has arrived,
Yours is the destiny to ride with the king,
And see his majesty to the edge of Nando,
That the harvest of the land shall tarry no longer.

My heart of hearts, the strength of my arm,   30
Ours is the union yet not consummated,
The cloth on the mat remained unrumpled,
The lamppost remained unoiled,
The new coiffure sits like a princess' tiara
On the head without the comfort of the husband's
Sweaty fingers dancing gingerly in its rows.

What is more? What about the gropes in the dark?
To search for the loose end of the wrappers?
Depart not my lord! Let another ride with
the king.   40
Abomination! What evil issues from your
mouth?

I am Shishi Atobe and I shall ride with his majesty,
The decision is not mine but the ancestors'
The legs are light, but the load is heavy,
It did not spoil at the time of Agbu,
It was not contaminated at the time of Angulu,
It must be lifted just as my forebears have done,
I am Shishi Atobe, I ride with my lord before dusk.

APAJUKUN:

"Our corn! Our beans! Our groundnut!   50
Where do you go to our lord?"
Apajukun, his majesty goes to return,
Apajukun, the vicar of the gods enters the sky
To converse with Chido to return with abundance,
Make way! Give way! Make way!

Be calm on the saddle dear majesty,
Nando calls from the east,
Khi'ndo beckons underneath.
They saw an effigy, but I felt a father,
The grandfather waits for the man,   60
And the ancestors are readied for the king,
Be calm on the saddle dear king of the corn harvest,
Shishi Atobe takes you to the place of red worms.

APAJUKUN:

"Our corn! Our beans! Our groundnut!
Where do you go to, our lord?"

"Our rainmaker, leave not your children with an
empty barn,"
"Take not the corns for porridge or the beer grains
with you"
"A father leaves the household provisioned   70
before departure,"
"A husband fills the granary before a peregrination,"
"Our lord, our corn, leave not your children
famished"

Hearken to your people oh father,
You shall return but your children must not starve,
Give out from your abundance,
And let the land be sated at the hour of pains.

TO THE PEOPLE:

I am Shishi Atobe and I hold the leash of
the royal mount,   80
His majesty ordered my stop,
For the land shall not be without abundance,
And the people shall not be without the stored
plenty,
The corns rush from his majesty's **riga**
And the outstretched hands of his subjects shall
collect them.

APAJUKUN:

"Majestic father, vicar of the gods,"
"Our corn, our beans, our groundnuts"

"We give thanks for we are grateful" 90
"But depart not from our presence,
Let not the sun set in midday,
Do not let the locust visit when the cornstalks grow
ears."

"Stay with us our corn, depart not from us our
abundance."
"Safe journey our father, where you go,
we follow not,
"In our hearts of hearts, the truth remained
unfaded." 100
"The king shall return but the man shall
become one with Akhi."

The wilderness enveloped the equestrian pilgrims,
The edge of Nando receded as it beckoned for an
embrace,
"Why follow the King and his rider beautiful
Atoshi?"
"I am **Kenjo** and nothing is hidden from my eyes,
I witnessed the promises made under the
cotton tree, 110
And the vows exchanged at the twilit
junction,"
"Talk, daughter of the woman before you are
cudgeled towards Khi'ndo."

ATOSHI:

Mbadi'Ku, I hide in the shadow of the **Aku,**

Lord Kenjo strike me not for I make obeisance,
My devotion was accompanied by regular sacrifices,
What is life without Shishi Atobe?
If he departs for Khi'ndo, I go with him,
If he makes Nando his habitation, I inhabit   120
it with him,
The auricles in my heart,
And the ventricles of my soul,
Are forever locked with Atobe,
I journey with him to the place of the king's rest.

KENJO:

Atobe, the king's horseman,
Nando neared and the denizens waited for the horse
and its riders,
Atoshi, your foolhardiness rankled Chido in
the depth of the skies,   130
The destiny of Shishi lies beyond Nando,
His wife called for his return to Khi'ndo at this hour,
Return, Atoshi, return to your kindred,
For Atobe's journey has just begun.

ATOSHI:

Shishi is promised to none except me,
I am his thighs, and I am his bosom,
From the abundance of my chest
He shall have the early milk,
This belly carries his germinating corn,
I am his mollification, I am his endearment,   140

His consolation, I am the rain on his parched earth,
After a long drought,
The kindled flame in the hut of the hearth of cold
ashes.
Dear deity, stop me not,
For the soul of Shishi calls out in the distance.

YAKU KEJI TO SHISHI ATOBE:

Who is the one who approached the citadel
of forested fear?

Who is the one who propelled stallion
hooves-   150
To the feast of the foliaged apparitions?

"Shishi Atobe the son of Minjiyawa"
"I bring the King to Nando,
That the man may rest,
and the king may return with corns"
Shishi Atobe, the King shall not enter Nando,
But the man shall find rest before departing for
Khi'ndo,
You shall dismount and give up the King
 Before you reach the reeded edges of
Nando.   160
"I dismount with the King, oh mother Yaku
Keji,
Here is his whisk and here is his fan,
The urn of the innards and the gourd of the heart,

I remove the riga and the embroidered cap of the
state,
The king is with you and with me is the remains of a
man."

Shishi Atobe, Nando opens to the man and
to you,   170
And at Khi'ndo, **Ama** waited patiently to
judge.

The edge of Nando calls, my dear friend,
A king for once and a king among kings at Khi'ndo,
Nando, the place of rest,
Your grandfather, with outstretched arms,

*Addressing **Nani-To**:*

NANI - To I bring to you the grandson,
He died as a king but the king returns with
Yaku Keji,   180
Your grandson sleeps out an unending
harmattan,
NANI - To I have brought to you the grandson.
NANI - *To addressing the body:*
Births are similar, the slave and the free,
But denizens of the world made their own way.
Ancestors, fathers, and mothers departed,
You are the initiates, I am the novice,
Hills pregnant with secrets,
Show me the path to bring him to you.   190
Unconquerable cats that outlast the city

On the day of the siege,
Effrontery coursed through them
And they queried the ancients on what they had for
supper,
In the place of answers, their parents' cadavers
made an appearance.
Redundant is the bridge in the presence of the
buzzing bee,
Sorrowful it is for the farmer in whose   200
presence the Okra hardened,
I bring the remains to you,
While the dam of the eyes fails
And there is a teary cascade at the spillways.
The remains of the son shall not be the meal of the
vulture,
Neither shall the stiff shadow of the initiate be
wasted
In the dunghill for the delight of the
carrion-eaters.   210
Let his deeds rest in Nando,
And let his soul find justice in Khi'ndo.

Alas! Where is the ecstasy of the cultivator?
When the melon is wrapped in draperies of blood?
What could be more heinous than the transition
Of the youth in the presence of elders?
The boa leads not its young to the scene of the hunt,
Dead leaves do not adjudicate a land dispute and
Spend the night at the frontier,
I shall depart and you shall find rest in   220
Nando,

And wait for all to meet at Khi'ndo.

Nani-To addresses Atobe:

Shishi Atobe you have not betrayed your ancestors,
You shall traverse not the road you came,
But shall journey along the banks of Sithi,
And cleanse yourself while showing your back
to the salutations of the weeping apparitions,
the horse is for Nando, but you are for your
homestead,   230
Go Shishi Atobe! Go!

*Meanwhile, Atoshi waited for Shishi at the Edge of
Nando and due to tiredness, she fell asleep.
Towards the first lights of the dawn, she was
woken by Kenjo, the deity of war.*

I, Kenjo the one not met by an acquaintance,
And the one found by the ignorant,
What is that sleeps in the clearing if not the meal of
the gods?

The house rejected it and the road collapsed   240
upon hearing its arrival,
What is it if not the deceasing of the unfortunate?
The journey to the city of no relatives
And the visit to the place of no siblings,
Another name for the one with the unfortunate lot.
The inside of the house of sleep is the untouchable,

But what wastes outside of it becomes a free game of the hunter!

ATOSHI RISING:

Stop Kenjo! Have you not heard?
They folded like a porcupine and turned the   250
head of the masquerade to an abode,
They warned of enemies in the front,
But the reply was that the rattlesnake's venom is in the front,
To be deployed for the swift death of assailants,
They told him of the confab of the betrayers in the rear,
The reply was that the scorpion's sting is in the rear,
Giving stealth death to the evildoers,
They warned of opposition in the middle,   260
He replied that to the left and right flanks
Does the thunder-deity vomit fiery hell,
For **Achu Nyande** knows not the neutrality of the fence-sitters.

I become the mountain and I remain solid and unmovable,
I have harvested the leaves of artful-death-dodger,
Hence, I shall live and shall not die!

Nothing shakes the heavens,
The river does not give fish head-porterage,   270
The presence of a coronet on the head of the vulture,

Gives it immunity to death and pestilence,
We do not see the hornbill bedecked with an agate-
bead necklace
And call for its execution,
No! The presence of a bracelet on the leg of the
parrot
Signals the commutation of the death
sentence,   280
What can the cock do to the bottled corn
other than staring?
Today, freely I walk, for I am not the food of
wandering deities.

KENJO TO ATOSHI:

Your words are the pronouncement of the gods,
For this, you shall be free of curses,
Now, that which you find walk by the Sithi,
He returns not this way,
Go to the **Sithi**, walk its banks,
There you shall find the desire of your   290
heart.

PART II

Shishi Atobe walks to Wukari by the way of the banks of Sithi. He hears the voice of his late wife, Akeh call out to him from the other side of the river.

The secrets of the earth,
 unhidden to the heavens,
 I climbed to the highest
To reach the summit of the summits,
All I have seen,   10
Lips sealed till the end of days.
The clamber of the Ibex on the thorny steeps,
An ascendance of desire over torture.

Nothing is greater than unity with the gods.
Blood curdled and heart panted,
Atoshi waits at the dying hearth,
Loin cloths loosened,
For a love deserted for duty.

AKEH TO SHISHI:

Duty imposed seven earth seasons of wait,
My lord, seven seasons of the wait at   20
Khi'ndo for

Your arrival from the marketplace called earth,
How much longer shall I wait?

SHISHI'S REPLY:

Akeh, the passion of my eyes
The warmth of loins when dry winds from the north
assailed,
But unknown to me is your tarry,
Unremembered anymore is the pains of your
departure,
And unreckoned with is the time   30
That divides us like the length of the Sithi.

AKE TO SHISHI:

For those who inhabit time,
Where morning, noon, and eventide have kings of
their own,
Where days make seasons and seasons make ages,
It is theirs to choose that which to re-memory,
For much existence is pains,
And much of it is trauma.

But if at your side memory lapses,
And amnesia brings bliss after trauma,   40
All that remains at my side is memory,
Memory, amid unchanging seasons of Khi'ndo.
Memory, in the stationary river of separation.
Memory, in the stale twilight of eternity.
Memory, in the fixity of limbo.

Memory, in the permanence of timelessness.
All that is left is memory.

Memory kaleidoscopic and picturesque,
And out of many colours,
What jarred and ensured the wait: 50
The promise of eternal love, made under
the canopy of the Bayan,
It kept lighted the only flame in the reverie called
Khi'ndo.

SHISHI REPLIES:

An oath made while the Bayan witnessed,
The concordance of two pulsating hearts,
Except for the buffoon! Who forgets the whispers
made
While the gods eavesdropped?
Akeh wait no more,   60
Akeh tarry no longer,
Let Khi'ndo no longer be in haste,
Let Khi'ndo open for the new inmate,

AKEH TO SHISHI:

The door of Khi'ndo opens,
Lost is the key to the earth.
*[He steps into the River Sithi and moves towards
the direction of Akeh's voice]*

ATOSHI ARRIVES:

Abomination! No one hears the voice of chaos
At the conference of the masquerades,
The movement forward is impossible,   70
Hence the inevitability of retreat!
When the Iroko is summoned,
It accepts appeasement.
Life and the world and its fullness belong to you
Shishi,
And entrance into Khi'ndo: a vanishing point.

AKEH REPLIES TO ATOSHI WHILE SHISHI
STOOD KNEE-DEEP IN THE RIVER:

Two hundred horned buffalos!
It's time to go berserk,
The earth opens once and it swallows,
Shishi! Step forward!   80

ATOSHI TO AKEH:

Impossible! The earth chose vastness without limits,
Hence its many watering holes,
Parrots! Come take my voice
To the front yards at **Kona**
Where there is the felicity of the avian mothers.
Be convinced today and forever,
That the porcupine is not a member of the portable
preys,
And when the cat perches on the roof,

It sees the whole yard and the extremities of   90
the wild,
The gust whimsically tosses dead leaves in the
directions of its choice,
Today I toss Shishi in the direction of the living
world!

AKEH TO ATOSHI:

Stop your noise! The banter is over,
Courage is for the external
But caution is for the home,
They viewed the dead with the eyes of the
past,   100
Hence their undressing by an apparition.

ATOSHI TO AKEH:

Shut up and keep silent!
'Clarify it' is the cry of the drum in the city of the
king,
For you it shall be made clear:
A woman is ungrateful,
Because her lived existence knows not the mystery,
No one can tell if her ghost can identify the fearsome
apparition,
For this reason, she daily seeks that which   110
is not lost!

You are a day-old pup, hence the whining you
mistook for barks,

A mere foal, hence, the clumsy stagger you called a
gallop.

One does not have sixteen elders within reach,
And seek counsel in the public square.
Unknown to the stranger is the footprints of the
natives,
Hence his arrival to the town at the hour of   120
the dark.
Now listen! when the river flows it does not look
back.

The whole of the living humans is the abomination
of the toad,
When the dog dies, it becomes separated from its
collar,
Shishi belongs to the side of the living,
He is separated from you,
And your wait becomes futile.   130
Now hear this: sleep is the one who
snatches the plaything of a clingy child,
I command you to sleep!

Sleep and find rest till the day when **Ama** rouses all,
Sleep!

[*All became silent. Shishi snapped out of reverie
and moved frightfully out of the river*]
Atoshi! Why are you here?

ATOSHI TO SHISHI:

The toddler knows nothing,
The body is unhidden to the sponge,   140
Come quickly, come over,
Life calls in the distance,
Here is the place of many hauntings,
Come with me and let swiftness enter our legs,
Let us hasten to leave Sithi the companion of
Khi'ndo,
Come with me Shishi, come now!

[*They ran very fast to the path that
led to* **Wukari**]

Ours is the union of the living deities,   150
Let all evil desist from our homestead,
And let all harbingers of catastrophe be
blinded to our hearth,
As we walk to the love of the ages,
Let the earth not heat under our bare or
sandalled feet,
Let all disease hear the call of another place
and not our own,
For we have made a pact with longevity the
duke of wealth,   160
Shishi, Atoshi, ours is the union of the
deities.

AFTERWORDS

It is well, all is well that ends well,
New corn sprouted in **Wukari**,[22]
New harvest entered the barns
And fresh **burukutu** was brewed,
Aku Uka ruled, and corn became abundant,
Apajukun shall not be orphaned,
It is well, all is well that ends well.

---

[22] Crowning of the New King, Aku Uka at Wukari, the capital city.

ANYAꞶU

At my arrival, the whole city embraced silence.
It seemed like a bad joke, but there is no sign
of mirth.
It seemed like cheap buffoonery, but lips are not
creasing in laughter.
I am the face of the sun, I shall know no eventide.
Who are the inhabitants of the place of shifting
cemetery?

Where straying ghosts made drunken
walks-   10
upon fluffy balustrade?
Fluffy balustrade, that made obeisance to
noon-day apparitions?

They assembled for the communion,
Communion at the place of deserted anthills,
Deserted anthills whose occupants are the
Starved ancestors and flightless fairies.
Who convened the meeting of divine malcontents?
No one else but **Ekwensu**,

Ekwensu, the occupier of idle hands with   20
entrapment.

They sought the blanket of the dark for their deeds,
Like harried bats, they whimpered,
They scurried when they heard the footfalls
of the dawn.
Beloved Anyanwu,
What the eyes have seen,
The mouth's forbidden to tell,
What the ears have heard,
The tongue must not relay.   30

Beloved Anyanwu,
Like harvest-time fulfillment,
Your strident call made mothers hopeful,
Like whipping rains on parched and famished
soil,
Your presence brought delight-
To the thatched-roof fortress,
Where crimson sunset-
Tells the stories of panting maidens,
Panting maidens whose deft hands-   40
Guided coquettish lovers to
The edge of the abyss,
Abyss or paradise?

Who can tell the difference nowadays?
Anyanwu our beloved,
The jewels of the earth does not have
The sparkles of the sun,

Nor the brilliance of thy splendor.
Precious Anyanwu,
Let us merry, 50
Let us rejoice,
For you are with us at this time.

FØR ŦHE ŦⱲINS

Ejire the indigene of Isokun,
Magnificent **Edunjobi**!
Edumare gift me twins
That I may name them Taiyelolu and Omokehinde!

I have decided to favour two,
I have desisted from helping one,
Thus it was divined for Omokehinde,
When she was embarking on the journey-
To the citadel of humanity
From the citadel of heaven,   10
She was told to sacrifice two snails, two
bush rats, and two millipedes,
So that she can have company in her sojourn among
men,
She did as she was told
She had company, she did not walk alone!

In the womb, she had company,
In the cradle, she had company

In the winding bush paths, she was not
alone.   20
Omokehinde where is your companion?

'A few steps behind' the reply
Breathlessly, Taiyelolu made an appearance.
Omokehinde! Taiyelolu!
They journeyed in a company,
With children, with husbands, with friends.
For this, Omokehinde thanked the initiated,
The initiated thanked **Agbonmiregun**!
I blessed two,
I have desisted from favouring one.   30

ODE TO DESIRE

It's time dear Bacchus,
 The palm-wine for a change,
 And let the grapes be.
Bring Epicurus to **Iya Basira**
And let us treat divine palate to
The bolus of pounded yam,
Slivers of lettuce in grounded melon seeds-
Stewed in screaming oils of the palm,
And venison from the single shot-
Fired in the primeval forests.   10
Leave your Olympian heights!
'Tis only to early callers
That Iya Basira caters to.

Listen to your fate,
The coin was given to bony fingers
At the time of the morning
Whilst you are not mourning.
Like the calvarial cross,
You bore the curse.

Like the bound slave,   20
You carried the brand.
My oracle speaks-
Greater truth than the Delphi's.
It is your fate to chase that which you hate

Vestal virgins, it's time for sacrifice.

Phallic knives throbbing on hymen gates.
Fear not thou maidens of the Lost Souls!
This night, your penitence shall redeem-
That which was lost to impatience,
Hmm, the impatience of the loins in agony   30
Hmm, the impatience of a lone night of sin.
Put on your whites, oh maidens loft,
If there be among you whose chaste is suspect,
To those that believe, their sins are forgiven.
The knives are ready for willing gates,
Open up and let them in,
To those that believe, their sins shall be forgiven.

Heaven's gate was sighted
In the brief moment of whiteness.
'Tis like eons that we entered through the   40
pleasure gates,
'Tis like ages when that which was wrapped,
That which was wrapped delicately like **Moi-Moi,**
Was pounced upon and torn in a single second
Of ravenous hunger.

Rivulets of salty liquidity cascaded down twin
goddesses
Holy Mother I have confessed my sins!
I shall no longer walk the dark mazes of
endless corridors,   50
I shall no longer beat dirt path to death,
Even though the kingdom is not thine,
Nor the power yours,
But your buxom beauty is the envy of the gods.

Oh sad minstrel playing soul ditties
Arcadia left just before dawn.

Is it Arcadia or Ile-Ife?
'Tis Ile-ife before the deluge.
But she left before the dawn.

And your love songs meant nothing,   60
Nor the bouquet of flowers from the wild,
Meant anything to the material sweetheart-
Of shopping mall street,
She smiles at your songs thought you,
But her mascaraed eyes missed not the tarred road
Nor her ears desisted from cupping the blaring
horns of wheeled monsters.

Soon and very soon she's going to meet
the king!
The king with the pregnancy of crisp notes -   70
In need of a midwife for safe delivery.
These crisps send her on a lyrical journey-

Much more rewarding than your penniless
composition.

But play on oh happy player and remember:
Arcadia left just before dawn.

All are fleeing ecstasy and fleeing ecstasy, all.
I am the prophet of your fate.
And it is your fate to chase what you hate
From now till the end of time.
If there is any time such as that.

80

SAINT VALENTINE'S
DAY ECSTASY

Like the sonorous beats of **baata,**
  I shall accompany your swaggering steps-
  To the altar of unity.
Where ecstasy is assured,
The maddening world
Placed behind damask drapes. For the moment.

Young love, young lovers,
What a delectable sight to behold.
Hah! Happiness and expectations.
Hah! Kindling fires at its bluest.   10
The two shall become one.

Hands clasped,
Bodies pressed tight on ***okadaic*** wheels,
Motion pulls them to wonder.
Young lovers, young love!

Many promises and greater disappointments,
When bodies age and the fire turns crimson.

Grip this moment oh happy children,
The promises of the bedchamber are-
More than its curses. It is true.   20

We shall send you ravens at seasons' end.
We have made the pyre. We bid you Godspeed.
The wood cracked under primordial flames.
You have become one with the deities.
Who are we to be anguished? We are shadows!
We, all, are striving shadows, soon to be darkened-
By twilight hues, to be silenced forever by the black
midnight.

We all strive. Like the hyacinth choked
riverbed,   30
'Tis the dead that mourns the dead.
And yet those who depart converse not with the
living.

Dear friend have your eternal rest,
And eat whatever is served to you at the citadels of
heaven.

Here lies frustration and failed expectations.
Once a bundle of life. Forever a heap of rubbles.

Are we not entertained? Let the dirges segue
Into a song of rebirth: "maestro, we have   40
ceased to be sad".

Our past died before it lived!
Is our future dead too?
Today angels are dazzled by your grace,
My lady, you are simply a dream to all beholders.
There are no warm beds in sepulchres,
Cuddling is for the living,
Kissing is for salivating mouths.
This is all that we have got. Tomorrow is
damned!   50

Obatala held a council in pristine Ife,
While Agamemnon belched on the Grecian throne.
The king of the white cloth still preaches love.
Let us depart now with the thought that-
Might is not right.

If I go before you,
Let your voice sing the gentlest of lullabies
To my departing figure.
But for now the bedchamber beckons.

PATH OF BONES

Like autumn leaves
They cracked under feet.
The faster the walk,
The more plaintive the cry
I can see you yonder oh gate!
Open the portcullis!

Black famished horses,
Eight stirrups astride,
Fast polished hoofs on bleached skulls.
Hot pursuit!   10
Sound the trumpet!
Prepare for the siege!
The enemy is at the gate.

The path of bones,
Memorials to waste,
Effigies of vanities-
Of days gone before.
Will the living learn?

Path of bones, Path of bones!

Like the slivers of shattered china,   20
Like the potsherds of the place of **apaadi**,
Disparate epitaphs to what once had care.
Who is the fool that wishes the-
Dead rest in peace? Who is the fool?
Generals command, the rank obeys.

The locust kings are at the gate,
Our commander is feasting.
They burned the crops,
They wasted the fields.
Our officers' gluttony climbed.   30

Come child, come to me.
To the sewers, we shall go.
This war our General shall not win.
The enemies' arms,
Not of greater fabrication.
Nor their men, of better motivation.
This war our General shall not win.

For the path of bones outside the walls,
Not of the enemies' dead.
But of friends and relatives.   40
They were citizens of the city
Who once told the Generals
That might is not right.
Let us burrow deep
Let us borrow sleep.
It is going to be a long winter.

Here is the thing that curdled the blood.
"He is a tree without roots"
The boy calls you father.
"He has been claimed. He is for death"   50
The boy calls you father.
"I am the man"
The boy calls you father.
"Not a son. Not from the loins"
The lass calls you father.

Father, great house,
Fortress in the day of adversity.
There is no father in this land
There is no mother in this place
Home and hearth laid buried in -   60
The fading pangs of torn embrace.
The spoken words of the covenant,
They must not be forgotten.
The silence of trust,
My father, my fortress.

Rivulets of sons course from the fathers' loins.
Did we suckle the same nipples?
Shared a crypt during the journey-
From the citadels of heaven?
Sons are more than what came   70
From a father's loins,
Blood is thick but-
A sleeping mat shared is thicker.
'Tis another's child that we give
a midnight assignment.

Towering like **Iroko,**
Graceful like gazelle,
Father, great house, a fortress.

Home is a fading mass of wistfulness,
Hearth lay buried in the rubble of distance.   80
"Father, father" The lad called
"She voted you father"
"You shall have no hand in his blood"

"...I will be faithful, I will bear true allegiance"
To the motor-park sleepers and the under bridge
citizens,
To the roaming and hungry scholars,
To the girls of threatened innocence
And the ladies of assailed virtues,
"I will be faithful, I will bear true allegiance"   90
To the stymied mothers whose lungs
bellowed,
Whose eyes drizzled tears from the blows of smoke,
When kindling flames for evening meals,
With neonates strapped to back.
"I will be faithful, I will bear true allegiance"

Only the father we can run to!
He is neither a king nor a priest.
He is the father to all,
The baobab tree with wide branches,   100
All can perch, all can trust.

"The gods shall be appeased"
"The boy shall die at dawn"
Hush! He is being led away.
He meekly walked like a lamb,
On his head, he carried the heavy load,
The burden is not his own, oh, not his own.

"He that carried a load that he is unaware of"
Hmm-Hah, what a fate!
"He carried gourds, he lifted enamel-   110
wares"
Hmm-Hah what a fate!
"She carried **ikoko** the father of all pots"
Hmm-Hah what a fate!
"She that carried a load that she is unaware of"
Hmm-Hah what a fate!

Cudgeled on the head,
buffeted with daggers,
"Are you the one behind me father?"
"Is the machete in your hand for my   120
enemies?"
"I run to you fortress, I call you father"
You are wrong lad,
I am no father of yours.

Machete to the jugular.
A nation is not family.
A nation is a place of conquest,
I bear allegiance to the self.
All hail the king, all worship his majesty.

QUEEN OF SHOPPING
MALL STREET

The vulture accepts all loads,
Hence its baldness.
Eshu accepted all the blame
And men were not wanting of follies.
Gilded grace, Doric columns,
Who shall accompany his majesty
To the upper chamber?
"Not you oh hag!"

Disposability is not the nature
Of that which shall grace the palace,   10
The woman who accompanies one
Home from a discotheque
Shall leave at the sound of a new ditty.
Queen of the Shopping Mall Street!
What passion craves it buys with its life,
Majesty was soiled by boiling boyish craving
For an appearance of the verdant.
'A single lover cannot fill the wardrobe'
Even a deity can be blinded.

Her laughter is the rupture of hyena,   20
In her eyes lurked the venom of the fox,
In her wake are bleeding rotting hearts,
Smashed into smithereens with her stiletto heels.
A lover cannot fill the wardrobe.
To the far reaches of the earth,
My pudding shall be served,
It is here, it is hot.
Be orderly in a queue,
There's enough for all with rabid desires.

Night arrived in midday.   30
Not even the gods can ascend my hills,
To taste in my avalanche of grace,
They must be supplicant, votive acolytes.
Abomination! Beaded-crown head whimpered,
Like a suckling babe, it sobbed.

The capitals of Bacchus lay at her feet.
'Business or pleasure, Madam?'
Blessed springtime carnations,
'Pleasure, always' in curt practiced dulcet.
There's no deity like the gullet,   40
'Tis daily it accepts new sacrifice.
The twig broke, and she flew,
Another branch in an instant distance,
Waiting for the perch of talons.

Homestead masquerades,
Farmland apparitions,
Four hundred and one that coursed
From the citadels of heaven,
Primeval mothers of the place
Underneath the twilight hues,   50
A son must not grace the market square
naked.

Queen of the Shopping Mall Street,
Glowing satin flesh not for groping lover's
caress in the dark,
'Tis only fit for glossy covers and velvet carpets.
Instant grammar or Instagram craves nothing
but drama.

Flowing taffeta like a whitened sepulcher,
Kept putrefactions away from lascivious   60
pupils.
'Are you not entertained?'
Never! Royal curves, please.
Smiles, smiles, smiles of the coquette,
Rabid desire can be smelt from afar,
Sizzling and hot is the pie,
A delectable whisper: 'come on over'
A wink across the 'gram,
Let's elope away from the reach of confused deities.

What passion craves it buys with its life.   70
A pout, a pose, click, send and slay.
Instant grammar, instant comments,

Four hundred and one Likes in the first second.
Lord *Eshu* told the others:
'Times have changed, let the Queen go for shopping'

ODUNMBAKU

Odunmbaku,
      My hen of redemption instead.
      In a fourscore lifetime,
Death visits thrice.
Odunmbaku,
The year death came calling,
A thousand and four gourds of herbs,
Two hundred deities stood sentinel.

The fire made for the vulture-
Ended up consuming the hawk.   10
Hands lifted by banana,
Used, pitifully, to flog no one but itself.
Death in the youth is an abomination –
For the hornbill.
The parrot does not trade its destiny
Of abundant life in the avian assembly.

What I knelt to choose is longevity.
On the day the road is thirsty,
I shall be found indoors with fever.
On the day *Iroko* shall fall due to   20

weariness,
I shall be in the plains with the maidens.
When **Lakaye** the iron-deity shall be on a
rampage,
When he chooses to set aside water and bath with
blood,
I shall be in distant lands, having traversed
seven mountains.

Ha! It's a lie! When they lay in ambush on
the usual path,   30
Whitlow on my big toe shall keep me
bedridden.
Lightning shall pierce the harmattan night
At the moment when the next step leads to the
abyss.

The poison mixed with my brew at the tavern,
To the latrine it shall pass, without hindrance.
At the council of the avian-mothers,
Like **Oduduwa**, the distinguished
mystery,   40
My case shall remain different.
Their **shigidi**, their hatchet-robot
Shall return to them with vengeance!
It shall empty the plague meant for my household
Upon their firstborn.
Odunmbaku,
When death visited,
'Tis my destiny to be in hiding,
Dwelling in the secret place of **Olodumare**.

THE SECRET PLACE OF OLODUMARE

Like an echo that travelled through the jagged
        mountains,
    Meandering and returning to the ears
For a time, this time and the time after,
The soul of the penitent flew the
Leagues across oceans of timeless vastness,
Across undulating meadows of darkness.
Lightning piercing through shy crevices
Beckoned towards settled destiny.
Oh, the magnitude of fear!   10

You are within reach, yet you recede,
Through celestial dark alleys,
Through marble catacombs,
Taverns under the streets paved with gold
Across seas of the blue furnace,
Within humid blackness,
And foliaged caressing darkness,
You are within reach,
Yet you recede.

Unquestionable **Olodumare**,   20
Timeless, formless divine!
Yellowish orbs of flames for iris,
Guttural thunder for voice,
Shall the penitent hide in you?

Grinning skulls on famished fields,
The world was laid to waste by their greed.

Vicars of the lies cathedral,
Time moved like quicksand,
Yet a thousand years still had to deceive,
To deceive the supplicants at   30
The temple for the stymied psychotics,
Where jaded lunatics queued under swinging
scimitar.

Dwellers of the secret place of the Highest One,
Let us find solace under the shadows of
Olodumare.

The fiery King of timelessness,
Who inhabits not the glitzed throne-room of a
trillion onyx columns,
But simply in the humid chill of the dark   40
multiversal arenas.

SERMON AT THE REVOLUTION CATHEDRAL

In the beginning was the end of days,
Unceasing iteration, infinite looping.
Lost paradise? Beulah cohabited with
purgatory
As live-in lovers, while the books were opened.

'All is madness!' says the Preacher,
Hear the sermon on the hills of rebellion,
Fathers ravished sons' concubines,
And old roosters slew teenage cockerels
For the sake of longevity amulets,   10
While mothers confabbed at millenarist
hills,
Calling for the visitation of thunder and brimstone
On the mighty hawks who are fattened
By the tender flesh of day-old chicks.

Befuddled agitators and praying mantises.
They sent reactionaries to the meeting of
revolutionaries,

Made free dealers the commissars of the
people's front,   20
So that the fire will burn itself out and the
beast will rule
For a thousand years and tell the people this:
there is no alternative.

Resignation to the antinomy called the twining of
wretchedness with wealth,
Or the deadly strive between brothers for the
master's beckon?

A beautiful sight in the delectable hills of
Great Beyond City,   30
Comrade Nkrumah, Comrade Lenin,
comparing notes in eternity,
'Comrade Lenin, I extended your argument and
postulated that
Neocolonialism is the last stage of imperialism'
'**Fantasticheskiy**! I wrote that imperialism is the
highest stage of capitalism'
Bravo! Bravo! Gentlemen, can both of you agree that
Neocolonialism
Is the highest stage of capitalism?   40

So many 'neos' disguising the old,
Neo-wine in paleo-skins or paleo-wine in neo-skins?
The sun has seen all things and failed to be
astonished.

Slaveholders were once liberals,

Gratuitously manumitted the ones they banished to
the bare life,
And kept the surplus value from tortured labour
In subterranean vaults.

Four hundred years of lucre made from   50
others' tears, sweat, and blood
Made capital's outstretched arms to encapsulate the
globe.
Grand eminence, you have a gusher in the desert,
Paleo-dromedaries drink water,
Neo-dromedaries drink hydrocarbons,
'God be praised, but where are the hydrocarbon
oasis?'

The past vanished and new coins coursed
from old mints,   60
Gold had vacation and paper-certification
of faith in the governments
Moved swiftly from the old vaults to the secret
numbered treasuries,
And the Grand eminence made ablution in the
Claridge's,
Was called to prayer at Credit Suisse,
And broke the fast at Daimler-Benz.

Hot money like molten magma,
Willing creditors befriended banana   70
emperors,
Khakied revolutionaries laced party-lines with
Gucci's quotes.

Once as paleo-liberals they held slaves,
Now they are neoliberals when amnesia dulled the
agitator's venom,
And extended stock options to the leaders of the
earth's wretched.

'Civilization is the enemy of progress,
And enlightenment is the sire of bestiality'   80
says the Preacher.
Jungled fathers sent sons to Oxford and Sorbonne,
The Whiteman is the god who coughed thunder,
The children must be like the new deity,
That our people may not be inmates of purgatory
forever.

'Wretches have no history, for history began with
writing'
Unnecessary debate, but the sons were
ensnared,   90
Hence the iterative proving; proving of the
proof
And proving after proving,
I shall prove to you that I am human,
I shall prove to you that I have history stored
in my head and not on papyrus,
I shall prove to you that I had emperors and
kings who ruled me before you came,
I shall prove to you that I built cities and
did not live on trees,   100
I shall prove to you that I was civilized and
had a glorious past.

The dialogue with stones is an unnecessary debate.

Sons of women, brothers of men,
The dominion moment asked a question.
That good fences might make good neighbours,
Many walls were made in a land whose houses had
no doors.

But the question remained unanswered,
While brothers begged the protectors for   110
admission into the courtyard,
So as to become the lords of the manor when
the old masters
Depart the jungle for the earned metropolitan
furlough.

Ile-Ife and **Arochukwu** had no doric-columned
tabernacles,
Yet Delphi's oracle spoke no greater truth than
Orunmila and *Ala*,
And Graeco-Latin Olympus had no greater   120
faculty
Than the four-hundred and one deities[23]
Who rained from the skies at the dawn of time.
Only if brethren shall desist from burning the icons
and effigies in the thatched-roof shrines,
And stop making us perpetual children of our
offspring,

---

[23] In Yoruba Mythology, the number of deities are said to be 401.

For it is from the black cauldron that the white
cornmeal emerges.

Upheaval calls for its birth,   130
Remove patronage from the metropolitan
diocese,
And let the disinherited brethren fashion declivity in
the plains,
And forge the roller-coaster descent into the
authentic hell.

Tired comrades and befuddled delegates,
The resilience of the empire and capital,
Buoyed by the love of men for class.
Labourers picketed but street-corner   140
capitalists smirked,
Solidarity? Never! We shall compete for the crumbs.
The sin is welfare, and the cure is enterprise,
They punished the wretched for loitering,
They shamed the poor for being broke.

Behold the abomination that birthed desolation,
The hero is the billionaire,
The deity is the market,
Both know it all and can do no wrong,
For if like **Dagon**, they fall,   150
They shall be rescued from the ignominy of
the crash,
So that the suppliant penitents shall not cease
At the votive-squares or is it the roulette parlours?
Any place where unfortunate heads can roll the dice,

While the house remained the only winner.

The queue is long, but they waited patiently.
Poverty became a disease, and the clinic had many
patients,
'Dear sir I pray thee, what is the cure for   160
the ailment that brought you here?'
One billion naira was the curt reply.
Be a billionaire and be cured of poverty.

The priests arrived and heaven started apartheid,
The poor and rich are separated at the pews,
All want to be a billionaire in a shantytown,
Gleaming Rolls-Royce Ghost rolling on potholed
laterite.

They saw the poor and declared him
unwelcome,   170
They saw the rich and they constructed
family trees.
The mad rush to insanity heated up the polity,
The pie is vanishing, but they claimed there is more
to be had,
The dough is shrinking but they said fortune favours
the swift,
The weak proclaimed virility and the poor had faith
and declared wealthiness,
And poverty eventually became the   180
unwanted bastard.

Oppression is the only game in the town,

In the town where everyone kept silent in the face of
tyranny,
For each of them wait for the time to accept the
obeisance of equals,
And to sit apart from the congregation on the high-
backed thrones.
Knowledge is cheap but it is seldom
acquired,   190
For it shines not like gold trinkets and
diamond brooches,
So unobtrusive like the dowager of yesterday's
potentate,
And yet as powerful as the rays called Gamma.
But without application, knowledge cools off like
lava.

Hence knowledge became the enemy.
They set out to clad the knowledgeable in
tatters,   200
And make the philosopher a Lazarus.
The lesson is learned, and the class is over:
Teacher teaching nonsense.
Oh prophet, heal thyself and cure your poverty,
For if knowledge is profitable,
Your mountain of minted wads shall seal the
mouths of dissidents.

'Knowledge for its own sake?' Jaded philosophy.
The egghead was left alone in the dank
office,   210
All roads led to the place of convocation in

Plato's old academy,
Where the heroic billionaire shall profess working
wealth,
And the pauperized academe shall certify
marketplace realism
With the standard of erudition: "Honoris Causa."

The curtains hid the puppeteers,
But the puppets are not without agency,
For there is a harmony of interests which   220
Makes the show an unending burlesque.
The puppets want irresponsibility,
The puppeteers want the eternity of globality of
serfdom.

Opposing binaries is their stability:
Black against whites,
Civilized against uncivilized,
Developed against underdeveloped,
Enlightened against savages,
The rich against the poor,
Men against women,   230
Heaven against hell,
Holiness against sin,
Thesis against Antithesis,
Words against opposites

Many orchids can bloom,
Finding harmony of colours in springtime orchestra.
A thousand flowers can bloom,
And the symmetry shall speak truthful beauties.

Babel is old fashioned in a world without
walls,   240
But if the colours of the rainbow resist
apartheid,
They shall be comforted in the knowledge that
atoms can be atomized,
And within colours, there are hues.
Workers of the world, disunite!
Each head must carry its own responsibility,
Why bargain collectively
When some of you are better than the rest
of you?   250
Why the solidarity with the wretched when
the elders' table beckons?

Why equality of reward when ability and effort are
unsimilar?
Workers of the world, compete!
Serfs of the universe, contend!
'Who is the Society? There is no such thing!'

For them to have a dagger at each other's throats,
A village became the assembly of
strangers.   260
Full-stomach blinded his eye so that
He may not see hunger the son of famished land,
Or see starvation the daughter of misery.
The market takes no notice of absentees,
They failed to compete and
They are visited by household famine.

Perpetual reforms, unending miseries,
Idleness found the rulers and the ruled,
For the rulers, dereliction of duty
Equals balanced budgets, 270
And irresponsibility means a surfeit of
loot.
But for the ruled: luck becomes manifest
Only in presence of the misfortune of their
neighbours.

The banana spoils but they called it ripeness,
The dough is shrinking but we engaged in free for
all,
Ensnaring brothers to purchase livelihood
With the gnashing of teeth of friends. 280
The time to return home has arrived.
The endured dilapidation has exceeded its carrying
capacity.
The deaf may have no ears to hear the
Dwindling footfalls in the market,
But when dusk arrives, he shall know
That it's time for departure.

The coming revolutions shall enthrone monsters,
But if happiness is what we seek,

It is time to let the earth heal by her 290
rulership of all.

GLOSSARY

1. **Apaadi**- It literarily means potsherd. In most contexts, it means the Yoruba equivalent of the biblical appropriation of Hades or underworld.
2. **Khakistocracy/ Khakistocratic**- Military rule, coined from the Khaki uniform of the Armed forces.
3. **Jumat**- Friday prayer. In many contexts, it signifies Friday.
4. **Alagbon**- Force Criminal Investigation and Intelligence Department [FCIID] of the Nigerian Police Force. It is in Alagbon close, Lagos. It is simply known as 'Alagbon' and it is an important police detention center and also notorious for human rights abuses.
5. **Ezu River**- A river in Anambra state. It became famous when bodies of young men, believed to have been victims of extra-judicial killings, were seen floating on the river in 2013.
6. **Eshu**- A major deity in the Yoruba pantheon of gods. He has been wrongly appropriated as 'Satan' or 'devil' in the Yoruba bible. He performs the role of witness and enforcer of oaths, divine laws, intermediary to the gods. He occupies the grey area of junctions and he is seen as possessing dual attributes. He is also a

trickster. He is popular in the Yoruba diasporic religions of Candomble, Voodoo, and Orixa as Esu, Papa legba or simply legba[legba is derived from full name Esu Elegbara].

7. **Ogun -** Yoruba deified ancestor who is credited with the invention of Iron. He is also seen as the god of war, and he is the patron deity of hunters, blacksmiths, and warriors. Nigerian Nobel Laureate in Literature, Wole Soyinka, conceived Ogun as the creative force in his poem, "Idanre".

8. **Kabiyesi -** It literarily means 'let us question him is unavailable.' It is a salutation used to praise and greet a Yoruba king. It signifies the termination of appeal, rather than an absoluteness of authority.

9. **Eweku-Elele -**This is the refrain used in the specific folktale narrated in the poem. It is used to achieve audience participation in storytelling.

10. **Ajanaku -** The praise name of Elephant among the Yoruba.

11. **Longę -** Stealth.

12. **Olokun -** The Yoruba deity of the Atlantic Ocean. He is closely associated with 'Ajé', the deity of wealth and commerce. The connection of the Atlantic Ocean with wealth suggests the participation of Yoruba in the Atlantic slave trade.

13. **Ekaabo -** Yoruba for 'You are welcome'.

14. **Akwaaba** - Akan for 'You are welcome'
15. **Akosua** - day name for the girl that is given birth to on Sunday among the Akan people.
16. **Aduke** - Yoruba female name. It means 'one who was strived to be cared for by others'.
17. **Agbonmiregun** - Another name for Orunmila, the Yoruba god of wisdom and the founder of Ifa divination system.
18. **Kh'indo** - In Jukun religious system and beliefs, this is the underworld. The equivalent of Hades, where souls wait to be judged. It is believed to be located under the earth's surface.
19. **Burukutu** - The bear derived from sorghum that is usually brewed by Jukun women.
20. **Apajukun** - The people of Jukun as a community. The Jukun are an ethnic group, chiefly located in present day Taraba state of Nigeria.
21. **Nando** - A forested area in Jukun culture area that is believed to be the resting place of the bodies Jukun king. A royal burial ground. It literally means 'house of sleep or rest'.
22. **Akhi** - The Jukun concept of personified ancestors. It also means physical death.
23. **Kenjo** - Jukun deity of war.
24. **Mbadi'ku** - 'I rest in the shadow of the Aku'. It is the declaration uttered by the any Jukun person to an assailant or a person that wants to hurt or punish him or her, so that the person may desist because the weaker person has

figuratively sought cover in the domain of the King.

25. **Aku Uka** - The Jukun priest-king and paramount chief. He is seen as the intermediary between the people and the departed ancestors. He is also seen as the living deity who guarantees the fertility and harvest of the land.

26. **Yaku-Keji** - A Jukun female deity. The Jukun seek her help at the time of drought, famine or any impending national threat.

27. **NaniTo** - The priest in charge of Nando.

28. **Sithi** - The mythological river believed by the Jukun to separate the world of the living and Khi'ndo, the underworld.

29. **Achu Nyande** - Jukun's god of thunder.

30. **Kona** - a town in Jukunland.

31. **Wukari-** Jukun's capital city and the location of Aku Uka palace.

32. **Ekwensu** - Igbo trickster deity, god of warfare and witness to negotiations. He has been wrongly appropriated in the Igbo Christianity as satan.

33. **Ejire** - Yoruba word for twins.

34. **Edunjobi** - Yoruba word for twins.

35. **Edumare/Olodumare** - Yoruba conceptualization of the supreme God.

36. **Iya Basira** - Mother of Basira, figurative persona of the female food vendor in major

Yoruba cities whose food is tasty and inexpensive.

37. **MoiMoi** - Beans pudding. A common Yoruba food.

38. **Baata** - A type of Yoruba drum.

39. **Okadaic** - adjective coinage from the word 'Okada', a town in Edo state, whose name has been appropriated by people of Lagos to mean the motorcycle taxi that became both commercial success and the means to navigate the ubiquitous Lagos traffic-holdups by persons who want to get to their offices early or meet important appointments.

40. **Iroko** - Milicia Excelsa.

41. **Obatala** - A deified ancestor among the Yoruba. He is believed to be the leader of the autochthonous group in Ile- Ife who was defeated by the Oduduwa group. Due to his acceptance of meek defeat and lower position and not seeking to right wrong with a civil war, he was deified as the god of peace and his symbol is the white cloth.

42. **Ikoko** - Yoruba word for earthenware pot.

43. **Odunmbaku** - 'The year I would have died' [Yoruba]

44. **Lakaiye**- The appellation of Ogun.

45. **Oduduwa** - Yoruba deified King. He imposed his rule over autochthonous groups in Ile Ife. He is credited to have started the centralization of power.

46. **Shigidi** - Figurine, usually carved from wood or made from terra-cotta. The Yoruba believe that a shigidi can be infused with malevolent spirit which make it to move like a robot to do hatchet jobs on another person.

47. **Fantastichesky** - Russian for 'Fantastic'.

48. **Orunmila** - see Agbonmiregun.

49. **Ala** - Igbo deity of the oracle of the hills.

50. **Dagon** - The philistine god in the Bible [I Samuel, 5] whose limbs were broken when it fell in the front of the Ark of the Covenant. This signifies the bowing down of lower power to a higher power.

51. **Ilyushin** - Russian Brand of Helicopter. It was manufactured during the Soviet Era.

52. **Mikoyan MiG** - Russian brand of warplane. It was manufactured during the Soviet Era.

53. **Ejigbomekun** - A market in Ile-Ife in Yoruba mythology.

54. **Puje** - A shrine in the outskirts of Wukari.

55. **Riga** - Aku Uka' tunic.

56. **Ama** - Jukun female deity and the keeper of the underworld.

57. **Ile Ife** - A town in Southwest Nigeria. It is acknowledged as the cradle of Yoruba cultural community and the home of Ifa Divination.

58. **Arochukwu** - A town in Southeast Nigeria. It is acknowledged as the home of the oracle of the Chiukwu.

APPRECIATION TO THE FOLLOWING GHOSTS

1. Fela Anikulapo Kuti,
2. Funmilayo Ransom Kuti
3. Chima Ubani
4. Dele Giwa,
5. Gani Fawehinmi,
6. Franz Fanon,
7. Harriet Tubman,
8. Martin Luther King,
9. Patrice Lumumba
10. Thomas Sankara,
11. Jean Baptiste Sans Souci,
12. Jean-Jacques Dessalines,
13. Toussaint Louverture,
14. Francois Capoix,
15. Kwame Nkrumah,
16. Malcom X,
17. Walter Rodney,
18. Bola Ige,
19. Steve Biko,
20. All the victims of the Atlantic Slave Trade,
21. All the civilians that were killed in the struggle for democracy in Nigeria,
22. All the civilians that were killed in the Nigerian Civil War.

Made in the USA
Las Vegas, NV
24 March 2022